I would recommend this book to nearly everyone. All of God's children have suffered or will suffer while in this present world. I found the book to be real, honest and most of all theologically correct. It has been my experience that most Christians do not understand how God is present with them in the dark places of life. They blame God and misunderstand God's presence with them. I love this quote from Nancy's story, "God weeps when I weep. God suffers when I suffer. And somehow, mysteriously, God works in me, and in so very many others who know life's tragedies, to turn suffering into service and evil into good."

-- Rev. Diane R. Cox, Staff Chaplain, WakeMed
Cary Hospital, Cary, NC

From the very first page, John Baggett draws you into a world of tragedy, faith, and hope. Masterfully intertwining both psychological and faith based perspectives, Baggett peers into the lives of those who have struggled against all hope. Whether working through your own tragedy or seeking help for others, Times of Tragedy and Moments of Grace will bring you comfort, understanding, a sense of fortitude, and peace.

--Dr. Margaret B. Patchet, psychologist and Dean
of Academic and Student Affairs, Cabarrus College
Concord, NC

It is a useful, readable, practical and spiritually and psychologically balanced book about every day faith and personal crises, written for and from the crucible of real life and not some "Reality Show". It's the "Real Deal."

-- John Freer MD, psychiatrist
Hopkinsville KY

John Baggett touches tender places in readers of Times of Tragedy and Moments of Grace. This book fills an important gap in addressing real issues of hurting people. Every person will benefit from this engaging and practical writing. Professional and lay care providers will want to share this book with those experiencing the pain of loss and the need for support.

As a retired pastor and hospice chaplain I appreciate the meaningful way that profound insights of social science are connected with sound theological and faith understanding. This is a valuable tool for hurting individuals, support groups and church school adult classes. Every reader will identify with the stories shared and find help from the faith resources offered.

--Rev. David Hilton, retired pastor and hospice
chaplain
Lebanon, OH

Those who have endured their own dark night of the soul will find this volume extremely helpful. And those who have not been laid low by loss but who suspect — correctly in most cases — that their time is coming will also be helped. After reading this book they will be better prepared for the disorientation, anger and readjustment of faith that are part of severe grief. One of the author's interpretations of the cross that I appreciate is this: It teaches us that the path to a faithful and satisfying life does not lead around pain, but leads directly through the pain and loss that always accompanies our efforts to love.

--Rev. Dr. Jack Good, pastor and counselor
Roanoke, VA

There are times when we psychiatrists find our diagnoses and evidence based treatment responses peripheral to a patient's experience of loss. The questions of "Why me?" and "Did I deserve this?" take center stage. John Baggett's broad experience has allowed him to assemble a book that engages these questions of ultimate meaning in a way that would allow us to recommend him as a counselor to our patients. Times of Tragedy and Moments of Grace carries its readers forward in a way that is honest and comforting without flinching away from the reality of pain. It is a book that belongs on every psychiatrist's bookshelf, ready to offer at a time of such need.

--Kenneth Gilbert MD, psychiatrist,
Champaign IL

TIMES OF TRAGEDY AND MOMENTS OF GRACE

John F Baggett

Outskirts Press, Inc.
Denver, Colorado

Outskirts Press, Inc.
http://www.outskirtspress.com

ISBN: 978-1-4327-4616-2

Library of Congress Control Number: 2009932956

PRINTED IN THE UNITED STATES OF AMERICA

Contents

Preface

I have known several times of tragedy in my life. I have also experienced many moments of grace during my seasons of grieving. This book has drawn significantly on those difficult times. And it reflects my own journey of faith in the midst of them.

Times of Tragedy and Moments of Grace also has been inspired by the struggles of many others. I am particularly indebted to the members of NAMI of North Carolina, especially those who shared their personal stories with me while I was working during the nineteen eighties on my doctoral dissertation titled *Self-stories and Coping Styles of Families with Mentally Ill Relatives*. I am grateful, as well, for the insights I have gained through the years from members of support groups and persons I have counseled. Deserving of special mention are the twenty-eight persons who participated in the grief study at St. John's United Methodist Church in Sebring Florida in the winter of 2009. Their personal sharing and insights during that pre-publication study of this book resulted in a number of important improvements in the manuscript.

I also have been blessed with some wonderful manuscript readers.

Rev. Diane Cox, Dr. Margaret Patchett, Sarah Gustafson, Diane Baggett, Rev. Ron DeGenaro, John Freer M.D., Rev. David Hilton, Rev. Dr. Jack Good, Rev. Charles Sensel, and Kenneth Gilbert M.D. each provided invaluable comments that have made this a much-improved book from the initial draft. In addition, my friend of many years, Michael Miller, as he did during the writing of my first book, *Seeing Through the Eyes of Jesus*, once again spent many hours doing fine editing, as well as providing substantive suggestions. It is difficult to imagine this final product without the assistance of each of these distinguished readers.

Finally, I wish to dedicate this book to the memory of my wonderful parents, John and Madge Baggett. While their deaths were difficult times of tragedy in my life, they each have occasioned many moments of grace throughout my personal journey, and continue to do so.

John F. Baggett
July 2, 2009

Introduction

"What I feared has come upon me;
what I dreaded has happened to me."
(Job 3:25 NIV)

The worst thing that ever happened to me did not happen to me. It happened to my son, Mark. In his teen years, Mark was a gifted and talented young man with a bright and promising future. On many occasions he expressed the desire to do something worthwhile with his life, and he often spoke of preparing himself for a profession that would help other people and make a positive contribution to society. I shared his idealism and his dreams. But at age seventeen, within a few weeks' time, everything changed.

Mark began to act strangely. He laughed at inappropriate times. He spent long hours in his room talking loudly and incoherently. He sometimes would approach me with wild eyes, to rant about a friend having used mental telepathy to give him a heart attack. And just when I thought things could not get any worse, they did. Mark began to have episodes of violent anger. He would break things and punch holes in the interior walls of the house. It was all bizarre and frightening. At first I did not know what to think. I suspected he might be on drugs. But I soon was to learn that my son had experienced the onset of schizophrenia, a brain disease that stole his personality and changed him forever. I did not know it at the time, but the tragedy of Mark's schizophrenia would change me forever as well.

After the onset of the disease, it was as though the son I had known no longer existed. In his place was another very different son, one who occasionally reminded me of the old Mark, but who, most of the time, was nothing like him. I grieved the loss of the child I had known for seventeen years, and I was filled with anxiety and anguish as I was confronted by the troubled soul who took his place.

Over the next few years, in response to my son's illness, I found myself experiencing, at one time or another, the stages of grief that Dr. Elizabeth Kübler-Ross identified in her book *On Death and Dying*. After the initial few days of emotional shock at the onset of his illness, I underwent, as so many grieving persons do, periods of denial, anger, bargaining and depression, along with what I believe to be other stages not identified in the Kübler-Ross model. As I suspect has been true for many others, these were not neatly defined progressive steps in my season of grief, but messily recurring moods and behaviors.

Although my grief was profoundly personal, it was not unique. As a reasonably observant human being, as well as one trained in theology and anthropology, I know that grief is a universal experience. People everywhere grieve when they have tragic losses in their lives. And every culture of humankind has recognized the value of the grieving process, and has developed socially acceptable ways for people to act when they are grieving.

Furthermore, while my grief felt as though I was on a dark, lonely journey, I was not the only one in emotional pain over the change in my son. Family and friends were also feeling the loss. Grief is a social experience. When a personal tragedy happens, it almost always happens to a group of people, even though it may affect some more harshly than others. Such shared events can create a fellowship of suffering, which, in turn, can make the pain of loss more bearable.

Grief also is a normal experience. It is a mistake to believe it can be avoided if we have enough strength of character, or enough faith. When we suffer a loss, whether we are among the strong or the weak, whether our faith is small or great, it is natural for us to experience grief. It is not a sign of weakness, but a manifestation of our humanity.

Grief is as necessary to emotional healing as physical discomfort is to bodily healing. Without pain, for example, we likely would not protect physically injured parts of our bodies long enough for recovery to occur. Similarly, the pain of a season of grief can serve as natural protection for our emotional injuries until they have time to heal.

The experience of grief is an integral part of life's spiritual journey. Whether or not we consciously realize it, the stages of grief are charged with emotional and spiritual significance. They reflect not only our changing relationships with our losses, but our shifting relationships with God as well.

We have navigated the journey of grief successfully when we have reached acceptance. Acceptance makes it possible for us to heal, to carry on with our lives, and ultimately to complete our journeys. As is true with physical injuries that disfigure and disable, emotional scars may last for a lifetime. Nevertheless, when we have been able to embrace and affirm our new reality, we are able to feel emotional and spiritual peace once more.

For me, as I struggled with my son's illness, acceptance was a long time in coming. I think that was true in my experience for two significant reasons. In the first place, my emotional energy, which was being consumed constantly by grief, was, at the same time, being taxed daily by the stress of the coping and adapting required when one cares for a seriously disabled family member. The second reason is that I am a person of faith, and my son's illness threw me into a crisis of faith.

I think I always had known bad things can happen to people of faith and to those they love. But I think I must have believed in my heart of hearts, for a very long time, that as long as I remained a faithful minister and servant of God, then God would put a shield of protection around my family. The tragedy of my son's illness shattered that illusion and laid bare the inadequacy of my naïve faith. I found myself journeying through a dark spiritual night, struggling with a new lucidity about life, and feeling overwhelmed by sadness. In the midst of my grief, my faith was tested profoundly as I struggled with an unwillingness to face and accept the reality of my son's condition.

The nineteenth century Christian philosopher Sören Kierkegaard wrote, in Fear and Trembling, the Sickness Unto Death, of the ways in which unfaith manifests itself at differing levels of consciousness when one is faced with life's difficulties. As I reflected on my own journey, Kierkegaard clarified for me that the stages of grief are far more than a natural healing process. He helped me see there are mortal temptations within each one. There are choices we can make, whether consciously or unconsciously, which either delay healing or prevent it altogether.

Kierkegaard helped me understand that people are living in unfaith when they reject the realities of their lives, whether those realities are experienced as blessings or as tragedies. To live in rebellion against "the way life is" is unfaith, because reality is created and sustained by that Mysterious Power we call God. It is God who gives each of us our lives, and it is God who places each of us in the midst of our unique circumstances and relationships in this world, a world where both blessings and tragedies occur. And it is God who continues to sustain us in life each day. Consequently, our relationship with reality, at any point in our lives, is a revealing sign of our relationship with God.

Certainly, an initial unwillingness to face reality, and the experience of time-limited episodes of the unwillingness to accept reality, can be

God-given phases of the universal journey of grief necessary in order for us to heal. And they can be important mileposts on the journey to a deeper and more profound faith. But when we adopt long-term strategies designed to avoid reality, to escape it, or to protest against it, I believe we are precariously at risk of falling into a life of unfaith. By making poor choices in our coping strategies, and by continuing in a stage of grief when it is time to move on, we can stray from the pathway to healing, and find ourselves in spiritual crisis.

With God's help, and with some assistance from Kierkegaard and others, I finally was able to recognize that my own journey through the grieving process was characterized, for the most part, by spiritual failure. That realization launched me on a quest to find a more adequate faith. While some of the emotional scarring brought about by my son's illness never would be removed, in time I received the grace to accept the inevitable and to undergo a spiritual renewal. And I was led to respond to a new calling, and to embark on a new ministry as an advocate for mentally ill persons and their families.

The most important thing for us to remember when dealing with personal grief is that we can get through it. The experience of grief, as painful as it is, is a mark of our humanity and a sign of our spiritual nature. It is a necessary journey for those who have encountered great loss and a prerequisite for those who hope to know joy and peace again. It is intended that the following chapters will provide practical and spiritual insight and guidance to assist persons devastated by tragic losses, to trust, with God's help, they too will be able to negotiate successfully their own most personal journeys.

In order to achieve this objective, the stages of grief and healing are explored in these pages within what I believe to be a more comprehensive and spiritually significant model than the one presented by Kübler-Ross. This model of the journey of grief in the context of faith begins with a Prelude in which the naïve state of faith is penetrated by tragedy, resulting in shock, fear and stress. This is followed by three major phases of spiritual struggle: (1) The Unwillingness to Face Reality, (2) The Unwillingness to Accept Reality, and (3) The Grace to Embrace Reality.

As the initial shock of a loss wanes, most of us go through a period of time when we are unwilling to face reality. We may attempt to cope with our emotional pain by going into denial, attempting to escape, or considering ourselves as victims needing rescue. Then, when the reality of our new situation breaks through these defenses, we usually enter a second phase, in which we are forced to face our losses, but remain unwilling to accept them. This phase, which often involves questioning, anger and depression, usually is the period of greatest emotional pain.

At some point, many of us, thankfully, will transition to a third phase in which we experience the grace to embrace the realities of our life-changing losses. We will come to know acceptance, a willingness to let go of the past, to change, and to heal. Some of us will experience our suffering as a calling, the willingness to transcend our own pain and personal desires in order to be agents of change. And, as people of faith, we may find ourselves going beyond simple acceptance to affirmation, to living in each moment and every season as God intended and assigned them to be lived.

It is important to understand that most of us do not experience all of the stages discussed here. Different people are prone to show preferences for differing types of coping strategies within each phase. It also must be emphasized that this model does not represent a predictable progression. Many of us cycle back and forth among the various stages, and between faith and unfaith, as did I. Unfortunately, as suggested above, it is not rare for some to become stuck in one of the earlier stages of grief, and to find themselves in the midst of a spiritual battlefield.

There is no standard time table for a stage of grief, though I believe most of us know, at some level of consciousness, when it is time to move on, when God is gently nudging us forward. Nor do I think our decisions to stay in denial, anger, depression, or one of the other stages prior to acceptance, are generally conscious ones. The temptation to become stuck in one of the earlier stages is, as so many temptations are, deceivingly seductive and subtle. One way I hope this book can be helpful, is by bringing consciousness to the journey, and awareness to the choices we face along the way.

Times of Tragedy and Moments of Grace is written for all of those among us who have had the illusion of protection from serious harm torn away by a terrible event. It is intended as a guide for those who need help in safely negotiating the crisis of faith that so often accompanies great loss, and in finding and developing the spiritual resources to survive the darkest days of grief and suffering. It is about the willingness to learn, to change, and to grow in the midst of life's difficulties, and about emotional and spiritual recovery from the devastating impact of troubles and tragedy. And it is a testimony to the mysterious power of God through faith to transform events that are experienced as radical suffering, and to use them for good.

Unlike a number of works dealing with faith and suffering, this book does not seek to explain the meaning of suffering by theoretical discussion of the problem of evil. Rather, it explores the journey of grief in the context of faith. Following a brief discussion in each chapter of a specific spiritual struggle in the midst of a particular stage of grieving, the reader will find a narrative that illustrates the forms of unfaith and faith that may occur along the path to recovery. The narratives dramatize ten different faces of tragedy.

Tragedy takes many forms, and the narratives contained in these chapters represent only a few. But those who have experienced other kinds of personal devastation are represented here, nonetheless. For all tragedies have common elements. All tragedies inflict a profound sense of personal loss and suffering.

Every reader may not agree that all the unfortunate happenings related in this book rise to the level of tragedy. Such perceptions are deeply personal. The loss of a job may seem, for example, to be a small bump on the road of life for some, while for others it is a major disaster. The reader, no doubt, will find some of the narratives contained in these pages to represent more profound tragedies than others. But that is also the way life comes to us. Some of life's valleys are deeper and darker than others.

Since this book primarily is written for a Christian audience, the chapters discuss the grieving journey from a Christian perspective, and the stories portray ordinary people from diverse Christian traditions who are confronted by extraordinary tragic events. But the chapter topics also mirror the universal human struggle with suffering, and they are presented in a manner intended to be of benefit as well to those who are members of other faith communities.

If you picked up this book, it is likely that you too have experienced a life- changing devastating event, or even a series of difficult losses in your own life. Perhaps you still are in a state of shock. Or maybe you are struggling through the stages of your grief, and searching to adapt and cope with the unwelcome changes that tragedy has imposed on your life and the lives of those close to you.

If your loss is recent, I recommend you not only read this book, but that you discuss it with others. Perhaps you can find a reading partner and the two of you can talk about it chapter by chapter. Or, as you proceed through the book, you may be able to share and discuss your thoughts and feelings with a pastor or counselor. Probably the most helpful way to study these chapters is in a grief support group or a church sponsored class in which readers can learn and grow spiritually as they journey together. And if none of these is a practical possibility, I encourage the reader, following each chapter, to write down thoughts and feelings in a journal.

Even if you have not experienced a recent loss, you may benefit from this book. Perhaps significant time now separates you from an event, but you continue to struggle with the relationship between the reality of that personal tragedy and the faith questions it raised for you. Or you may find yourself anticipating and worrying about a major loss that has not yet occurred. Alternatively, maybe you are not facing personal difficulties right now, but you picked up this book because you know someone who is, and you are uncertain about how best to help that person. If you recognize yourself in any of these situations, I have written this book for you.

Chapter 1:
Like Lightning Striking

"Moreover, no man knows when his hour will come:
as fish are caught in a cruel net,
or birds are taken in a snare,
so men are trapped by evil times
that fall unexpectedly upon them."
(Eccles. 9:12 NIV)

Shock

When tragedy enters our lives, it usually feels as if we have been struck by lightning. That is because such events tend to come to us suddenly, without warning, and they jolt us into a state of shock. This obviously is the case when the death of a loved one results from an accident or murder. But even when we expect a loss, as in a prolonged terminal illness of someone we love, we may be caught by surprise when the end finally comes, much as we can watch a storm cloud approaching, hear the rolling thunder, and, nevertheless be traumatized when lightning strikes our house or a tree nearby.

Human beings share a primordial fear that tragic things will happen. But most of us suppress our dread and live our daily lives believing such events are not going to occur, at least not today. If we did not set such fears aside, we likely would be paralyzed by them and unable to carry out the simplest of tasks. There are troubled souls who cannot ignore life's dangers and are crippled in their daily lives by raging fear. But most of the time, the rest of us are able to assume nothing bad is going to happen to us, and we are free to go about the business of living. Free, that is, until tragedy strikes in our lives.

Rachel

Nothing had prepared Rachel for what the doctor reported to her that day. The tumor was malignant, and the cancer was spreading throughout her body. Even with treatment, the oncologist predicted, she could expect to live for only about a year. The news threw Rachel into a state of emotional shock. She felt bewildered and disoriented.

It wasn't that Rachel was naïve. After all, she had been a nurse for over fifteen years. During that time, Rachel had seen many people die of cancer. She had, on a number of occasions, stood by the bed of patients and offered comfort to families as their loved ones passed on. She understood the biology of cancer and the physical and emotional toll it takes on patients and loved ones. She had witnessed it in all types of patients from many types of backgrounds. Intellectually she knew it could happen to anyone. But this was different. This was happening to her, and to those she held dear.

With the news there came a strange almost out-of-body experience. For a few moments she felt detached and uninvolved. Rachel had experienced this state of being only one other time. It had happened years before when she was riding with a friend on the Interstate in a freezing rain. The friend had tried to brake in order to slow down, but the car skidded off the road and down a long steep embankment. During those few seconds of uncontrollable sliding, before the car glided between two large trees and harmlessly came to a stop, Rachel thought she was about to die. Yet this thought was not accompanied by fear. She observed the entire event from the passenger seat as if she were in a tranquil dream.

That day in the doctor's office, she remained in a detached state as she checked out, left the office, and walked to her car. Then, as she was buckling her seat belt, a terrifying moment of lucidity rolled over her like a storm surge in a hurricane.

A curtain within her consciousness suddenly was torn apart, and Rachel found herself staring into a dark and bottomless abyss. Rachel always had known deep within herself that the abyss was there. But she also believed that somehow God would take care of her and never allow her to experience such an awful thing. "There must be some mistake," she thought. "This cannot be happening. It must be a dream."

In her years of experience, Rachel had witnessed many tragic occasions. She had come to believe that an event is tragic precisely because it is a wrenching loss of something precious. It might be the loss of security, or wholeness, or relationships, or hopes for the future. In Rachel's case it was all of the above, for she was dealing with a sickness she had been told would soon end in death.

In one moment, she had every reason to believe her life would take an expected course. She would live to see her children graduate from high school, and then college. She would see them fall in love and get married. One day she would hold her grandchildren in her arms. She would have many more years of a fulfilling and compassionate vocation caring for patients. As the years passed, she would continue to find ways to contribute to the work of her church and her community. She and David would grow old together and travel to exotic places. In that next moment, those hopes and dreams were gone.

Rachel had the presence of mind to know that she was in a state of shock. And her training made her aware that the shock of personal tragedy is a dangerous time. She thought about calling a friend to come drive her home. But against her own better judgment, she decided she would exercise extreme caution and stay off the expressway instead. Once on the road, however, she found it difficult to concentrate on her driving. Her mind kept rushing back to the conversation with the doctor and all of the accompanying fears. Then, without meaning to, she spaced out, thinking about nothing and no longer feeling anything. When it registered in her consciousness that she was pulling into her own driveway, she realized she had no memory of the trip.

Her house was empty and lonely. David was at work and the children were at school. For about an hour she walked in a daze around the house. Then her fear broke through her numbness. She found herself asking God, in a passionate loud voice, to please make it not so.

A little later, after several minutes of involuntary trembling, she decided it was not good for her to be alone. She desperately felt the need for her husband's comfort. She picked up the phone, fumbled with it, and finally dialed David's work number. She told him, between gasps for air, that she needed him to come home right away. But she refused, despite his worried questions, to tell him what was going on. David recognized that Rachel had been crying and that something was terribly wrong. He told his boss there was a family emergency, and hurried home.

Rachel met David as he came in the door. She threw herself into his arms, sobbing uncontrollably. He held her tightly and tried to calm her. After the sobbing subsided, David finally was able to obtain enough information to understand what was happening. They sat on the couch for a long time after that, while Rachel wept in his arms.

Rachel was fortunate that David was a loving, caring husband who understood the nature of the crisis he was dealing with that day. David had learned somewhere, probably in conversations with Rachel about her hospital experiences, that a person in emotional and spiritual shock needs assistance and support to get through the first few days. The wisest course for Rachel would be for her to have someone with her who could provide comfort, make mundane decisions, and assist with some of the activities of daily living. So David took a few days off from work.

Of course, David, too, was now in a state of shock and bewilderment. Rachel's news was the visitation of his worst nightmare. He could not yet fully comprehend what was happening to the love of his life and to his family. He needed those days off for himself as well, and he wanted to be with Rachel every second of the day.

Both of them knew this was not a time to make major decisions. That would come later. Neither was this a time to try to understand rationally the religious and spiritual significance of her condition. That, too, would need to wait. Yet, David also had a strong feeling that they both needed some spiritual help.

That evening, David called their pastor to tell him what was going on. The following morning the pastor came to visit. After expressing his sympathy to the couple and relaying the information that he already had activated the church's prayer chain on her behalf, he sat silently with them for a long while.

Finally, the pastor broke the silence. "I don't think anything I could say would be of much help today. I know you both are still in shock. This is not a time for us to try to make sense out of this frightening and awful news." "But," he went on, "it is a time for prayer, not prayers from the mind and the mouth, but simple prayers from the heart. At times like these, many people find the 'serenity prayer' to be the one that helps the most."

Then Rachel, David and the pastor held hands and together prayed:

"God grant me the serenity
to accept the things I cannot change;
the courage to change the things I can;
and the wisdom to know the difference."

After the prayer, the Pastor said, "During those times in my life when I have been shocked by some tragic news, I have found myself praying the first line of that prayer over and over. 'God grant me serenity.' 'God grant me serenity.' 'God grant me serenity.' Somehow I know instinctively that what I need most is to find some peace at my spiritual center. I need for the storm within me to calm enough that I can safely negotiate the time of shock and danger. I think the time when misfortune suddenly strikes is a time to remember and cling to familiar words, like those in the serenity prayer, that have been born out of the heartbreaking experiences of others."

As Rachel continued to reel in bewilderment those first few days, a series of agonizing thoughts ripped through her consciousness. "What about my husband David?" "How will he handle this?" "What about the children?" "What will they do?" "I am too young, and they are far too little for this to be happening." "And what about me?" she thought. "Am I going to lose my hair?" "Am I going to be in a lot of pain?" "How long will I really have before I am too sick to have any quality in my life?" Question after question came – only questions, with no answers.

In those moments, Rachel remembered to pray the serenity prayer. She prayed it over and over. She also found herself recalling some other familiar words – words from a hymn she often sang in church.

"When through the deep waters I call thee to go,
the rivers of sorrow shall not overflow;
for I will be with thee thy troubles to bless
and sanctify to thee thy deepest distress."
(From How Firm a Foundation, Author: Keen 1787)

The storm still swirled within her. Terror still gripped her being. But those words seemed to be something firm and stable amidst an emotional cyclone. She had been thrown into deep waters. She softly prayed for God's care and guidance for what was to come.

As the initial shock waned and the first rush of adrenalin drained,

Rachel realized she had some choices to make about how she would deal with her situation. Many years before, Rachel had turned to a supervisor for advice in dealing with a particularly difficult patient problem. "Let me tell you something that will save you a lot of trouble if you will heed it," her mentor had said. *"Your situation is never your problem. It is your relationship to your situation that is always your problem. No matter what your circumstance, the first decision you will make about that situation will be to choose the attitude you are going to have toward it. Once you have done that, you will know what to do."*

In her years of hospital work, Rachel often had observed that a patient's attitude had a lot to do with the outcome of an illness. She had seen some who chose to fight their diseases for as long as possible, and she had witnessed others who had surrendered to their conditions almost immediately. She had seen the way some patients chose to focus on their own misery. They became demanding and irritable with those around them, and made caring for their needs unpleasant for everyone. And she also had enjoyed taking care of some very seriously ill patients who remained cheerful, appreciative and sensitive to others. They seemed unwilling to complain, even when their conditions appeared unbearable.

Rachel also had been involved in several cases of inexplicable, even miraculous, recoveries. She believed she had seen first-hand the power of prayer and of a positive spiritual attitude in the healing process. She understood and took seriously what the physician had told her. Yet she also felt that only God knew whether there was a chance she could beat her cancer. And she believed that remission, even at this late stage in her condition, was possible. She knew that her church's prayer chains already had been activated, and that her colleagues at work were praying for her. Rachel decided to face the reality of her condition while steadfastly holding on to her hope.

Rachel thought about her husband and children. She thought about the patients and nurses at the hospital who still needed her services as a nurse manager. And Rachel decided that she was not going to be one of those people who just gives up. She knew the treatment for her disease would be incredibly uncomfortable. Her hair would fall out. She would experience constant nausea and weakness. But she was determined to do whatever it took to fight her disease.

The best-case scenario, of course, would be a cure, perhaps occurring mysteriously as what the medical community knows as a "spontaneous remission." Or perhaps it would come from a new medical breakthrough while she was buying a few more months with her radiation and chemotherapy treatments. Rachel decided she would hang on to those hopes as long as she could. But if, in the end, she still was going to die, then she was committed to squeezing as much quality out of life as was possible, and to being the best mother, wife and nurse manager she could be under the circumstances.

Rachel also decided that each day she would try to focus on the positives. She would attempt to stay grateful and pleasant in her attitude. She knew that if she did not survive, it would be unbelievably hard on those who loved her and depended on her. She wanted their burdens to be as light as possible.

Rachel had been told that as soon as she began treatments she would begin to lose hair. She decided to symbolize her intentional relationship to her personal tragedy by shopping for and purchasing an attractive wig. Then she went to the beauty shop, had all her hair shaved off, and began wearing the wig.

Having prayerfully decided how she intended to deal with her condition, Rachel asked God to help her remain faithful to the path she had chosen. As the weeks and months went by, some days were more difficult than others. But her family and friends all marveled at her determination and spirit. This was so even as she suffered through all her treatments, including a highly experimental one which made her especially sick.

Despite the side effects, the treatments slowed the disease and helped make it possible for Rachel to spend some irreplaceable times with her family. She and David took the children on a trip to the Grand Canyon. They attended a large family reunion. They spent almost every other weekend at their mountain cabin together. In the midst of all of this, she continued to work most days. She only took extended sick leave after fifteen months of battling with her illness. Despite her amazing faith and courage in the face of her devastating disease, her condition declined rapidly. Eighteen months after she had received the diagnosis from her doctor, Rachel died.

Rachel's memorial service was standing room only. She was remembered as a woman of faith who had faced her personal tragedy with great courage and grace. As her pastor concluded his message, he reminded those present that the sudden onset of Rachel's disease came as a shock to everyone who knew her as the youthful, vibrant person she was.

"None of us know," he said, "what tomorrow might bring. Such things can happen to any of us at any time, and when we least expect them. We can only hope that if and when they do, we will be as persistent in our hope as Rachel was. Until very close to the end, she held on to her hope for healing in this life. When it was clear that her time was drawing near, she held on just as fervently to her hope of heaven."

"Eighteen months ago, just after Rachel and David received the news of her diagnosis, I prayed with them in their family room. We stood together, held hands, and recited the serenity prayer. Rachel not only prayed that prayer, she also lived it. Throughout her ordeal, she remained a person of faith. She turned to God every day and prayed for the serenity to calm her anxiety, for comfort in the midst of her suffering, for courage in the face of her illness, and for guidance in deciding how to make the best use of each moment. She rejected self-pity and resentment as unacceptable options. She demonstrated a gentle and caring spirit in her relationships with those around her.

Throughout it all, she did everything she could to fight her disease, but she trusted God with the outcome."

"We have much to learn from Rachel. Her life instructs us on how to face disease and death with courage. But it also demonstrates how we can live wisely and authentically as people of faith."

Phase 1
The Unwillingness to Face Reality

Chapter 2:
Denial Is Not A River In Egypt

"When an overwhelming scourge sweeps by,
it cannot touch us,
for we have made a lie our refuge
and falsehood our hiding place."
(Isaiah 28:15b NIV)

Denial

Soon after we are struck by the initial shock of a life-changing loss, it is not unusual for us to enter a more or less extensive period of denial. When we are still in shock, disbelief can be a normal involuntary reaction. As this reaction begins to wane and reality intrudes upon our consciousness, we may attempt to perpetuate our disbelief for as long as possible.

At some level of our being we know the truth, but we are unwilling to face it. We assume by refusing to acknowledge it we are protected from its implications. And we attempt to convince ourselves it will be possible to continue to experience life much as it was before the tragic event occurred.

We sometimes will go to great lengths to defend and reinforce our states of denial. When the death of someone dear to us occurs, for example, we may expect the deceased to walk through the door at any time as if he or she has been away on a journey. Sometimes an extra place is set at the table. Closets containing a loved one's clothes may remain untouched. Bedrooms, particularly of children, may be maintained for many years as they were at the time of death. We may look for our loved one in a crowd of strangers and hope to hear his or her voice each time the phone rings.

Denial may soften the blow and postpone artificially for a time the overwhelming pain and devastating change in a person's life that comes with a loss. As such, it can be a temporary blessing. But it also carries with it great risks. Perhaps this can be seen most clearly if we think of a person who has a very serious physical symptom of some kind and refuses to see a physician about it. The illusion that the disease is not real unless it has been diagnosed is clung to for as long as possible. Not infrequently, such persons face serious disability or premature death which could have been avoided if they had sought help when the symptoms first appeared.

Denial can delay as well the interventions necessary to deal with addictions or marital problems. The unwillingness to acknowledge the existence of a problem has long been a key strategy of addicted persons for avoiding change. They continually work to convince themselves that they are not hooked on their drugs and that they can continue to abuse their substances without serious consequences. The first step toward any possible recovery for such a person is to admit that he or she is an addict. Similarly, the signs of an unfaithful spouse can be ignored for years, preventing the intervention needed for a healthy solution to an unhealthy relationship.

In hindsight, the clues will be obvious. But during the time of denial a person is unwilling to draw the necessary conclusions. That is true, among other reasons, because so many of us do not want to believe that we, or the people we deeply care about and live with every day, are behaving in a way that eventually will lead to terrible consequences. As long as the problem can be ignored successfully, the discomfort associated with intervention can be avoided. It is easier in the short run to live in denial than it is to face a problem and to take the often difficult and painful actions necessary to address it. But in the long run denial can be a recipe for disaster.

This is equally true for a person who has experienced the loss of a loved one. The longer we are in denial about the reality and implications of a death, the more unhealthy it can become for us. Death brings about the necessity for change in the lives of those of us who are left behind. It leaves a void in our lives. The person we have lost is unique and irreplaceable. The relationship we had, the time we spent together, and our mutual participation in activities and events cannot be duplicated.

The loss of those things requires constructive alternatives for how we spend our time and with whom we spend it. Sometimes the need for change in our living situation is urgent due to economic or safety concerns. In any case, prolonged denial prevents us from facing not only the loss we have experienced but the life decisions necessitated by that loss as well. As long as we maintain a state of denial it is unlikely we will be able to adapt successfully to our new situation.

While denial may have temporary psychological benefits, it can have emotionally unhealthy consequences as well. Denial is made possible by extremely fragile illusions that must be defended constantly, and repaired again and again in order to be maintained. Reality continually threatens to shatter the defensive shell of disbelief we have constructed. Tremendous energy and exhaustive psychological effort are needed to remain in denial for very long. Because we know at some level of consciousness that we are living a lie, we are possessed by fear and stress that over time can take both an emotional and a physical toll.

Fear is a God-given emotion that helps us to avoid danger and contributes to our survival in this world. But when fear takes charge of our lives, this God given gift becomes a form of unfaith manifested as a life filled with anxiety over all sorts of things, many of them of little or no importance. Jesus told his followers not to be anxious about their lives because such anxiety is a failure to trust God's care.

Similarly, denial is a God given coping mechanism that cushions the shock of a great personal loss. But denial can become a form of unfaith when it is chosen as a long-term strategy. Such unwillingness to face reality may indicate a lack of trust in God's ability as our Shepherd to see us through the dark valleys of our troubles. Consequently, our denial can delay and sometimes prevent altogether the healing God desires to bestow on us.

God is a God of truth. We are called by God to be truthful in our social interactions. We also are called to be truthful with ourselves. God is capable of helping us face the truth, no matter how horrible it may appear. And God is capable of helping us to adapt to the truth, no matter how challenging the changes which might be required in our lives.

Because God wants us to face reality rather than to hide from it, God seeks to break through our denial so that we might find healing. It may not feel that we are being cared for, but when the shell of our denial is penetrated and shattered, whether by events or by other people, it is God who is lovingly at work and is offering to help us to recover from our grief and to continue the journey we are intended to take.

Whether or not we recognize it as the activity of God, the time comes for most of us when the illusions that make denial possible are completely and irreparably shattered. When that happens, other coping strategies often come into play. But it is possible to become stuck in denial for a very long time.

Tanya

Tanya noticed that Keisha was a good bit slower than her other children had been. But she assumed her youngest daughter eventually would catch up. "Some children mature faster than others," she thought. "It isn't anything to worry about." But when the daughter started pre-school, her teachers suspected a problem right away, and ordered testing. The results sent Tanya into an initial state of shock. Suddenly, all the hopes she had dreamed, since Keisha stirred in the womb, had been dashed.

One day other children in the pre-school would go off to college, and then begin to live independent lives. But now Tanya had been told that Keisha would always be an emotional child with moderate mental retardation. Stunned, she suddenly had a vision of the future where she and her husband were sentenced to a lifetime of parenting and care giving. And the care would become more difficult with time and with age, until it became physically impossible. "Then what will happen?" she thought. She knew that many moderately mentally retarded persons live their adult lives in group homes that provide supportive care. But, at the moment, she could not bear the thought of Keisha living out her life that way. A profound sense of sadness engulfed Tanya. She felt cheated out of a daughter and out of her own life.

It was all too painful to contemplate. So Tanya stopped thinking about it. She refused to accept the results of the developmental evaluation. It was not a rational decision on Tanya's part, but it was a decision nonetheless. She went back to her usual daily routine. With grim determination, she changed nothing. She spent her days just as she had before. She got Keisha ready and drove her to pre-school each morning. She cleaned house, did the dishes, went grocery shopping, and talked to her best friend on the phone. She picked Keisha up from pre-school and met her two older children when they got off the bus. She made sure that any homework was done before they went out to play. She prepared dinner, got the kids ready for bed around eight, watched television, and went to bed herself around ten. Not once did she allow herself to believe anything had changed. Whenever she was asked about her daughter, she became irritated. But she managed politely to change the subject. After that first period of shock, she did not shed a single tear. After all, as long as everything remained as it had been, then there was nothing to cry about. Many weeks went by.

Perhaps things would have remained that way much longer, except for the fact that the pre-school director called one afternoon. She asked Tanya to show up for an emergency conference before school the next morning. At the meeting Tanya was told Keisha was so developmentally challenged that she could no longer remain in a mainstream pre-school. She could not keep up with the work. She had little or no impulse control. Both the teacher and the teacher's aide had been bitten by the child. In fact, Keisha had bitten the aide three times during a two-week period. The previous day had been a particularly disturbing one. Keisha had bitten two of her classmates, leaving serious bite marks on both of them. The parents of the injured children were furious. That was the straw that broke the camel's back for the school. Something had to be done.

Tanya attempted to reason with the teachers.

"She is only three," she said. "Lots of children go through a biting stage. I will talk to her about the biting."

The pre-school staff was not buying it. Everyone in the room knew Tanya already had been told about the biting several times and that each time she had promised to deal with Keisha's problem. Nothing had changed. The teachers also had attempted to deal with the behavior. But the child seemed incapable at this point of understanding that there was a connection between biting and a "time out." This was not a typical three-year-old behavior problem. The staff felt strongly that Keisha needed specialized services in a self-contained classroom with a special education teacher.

For the first time since hearing the results of the initial evaluation, Tanya felt a crack in her emotional armor. No longer could she successfully withhold all tears. From that point forward, she found it impossible to maintain what had been a virtually impenetrable denial of the reality of Keisha's condition. After an agonizing night, she informed the director of the pre-school she would agree to the self-contained class. It was not an easy decision. Tanya hated the thought of the new placement. It would label Keisha as mentally retarded, and it would mean less would be expected of her.

Tanya was not comfortable with her decision. But she made it. In her heart, however, she still hoped that the experts were wrong and that Keisha, with a little help, could grow out of this developmental thing. She was willing, for the moment, to recognize there was a problem, but she was not ready to believe it was going to be a serious and long term one.

Soon Tanya began to make the rounds of various pediatricians, psychologists, and child development centers. She was determined to find some authority who would declare the original evaluation wrong. In the process, she gained some new knowledge of her daughter's condition. But in the end, everyone agreed with the results of the original evaluation.

Next Tanya began to search the Internet for possible miracle cures. She looked into vitamin therapy and growth hormones. She even fed her daughter some natural supplements for a while, until she heard a warning on television about the effects of unregulated supplements on young children.

Week after week, she asked her church to pray for a miracle, so that God would heal Keisha's brain and cause it to develop normally. She even carried Keisha to a church over a hundred miles away, in the hope that she might be healed. The preacher laid his hands on the child and prayed, and for more than a week afterward Tanya believed it had worked, that Keisha had been cured. But the reality soon sank in. Nothing had changed. Keisha was still the same developmentally challenged child. Nothing was working. Tanya became even more frantic to find something to change the situation.

She prayed and prayed. In her prayers she tried to strike a deal with God. If God would make Keisha O.K., Tanya promised, then Tanya would give up deserts and shopping, or whatever else God wanted her to give up. She would give them up forever. She even offered to take upon herself some terrible disease or disability, if only her child would be made whole. She promised to go to church every Sunday, and to do whatever God wanted her to do. "Please tell me, God, what I have to do," she prayed, "and I will do it."

The answer to Tanya's prayer did not come as she had hoped it would come. After months of unsuccessfully trying to cut a deal with God, it did not come in the form of a miraculous cure. Instead, it came one night in the words of her husband, who had grown weary of the expenditure of time, energy and money chasing a cure that he had come to believe would never happen.

"You want to know what God wants you to do?" he asked. "I'll tell you what God wants you to do. God wants you to accept the fact that Keisha is retarded and will always be retarded. I'm sure God heals lots of people. Even the doctors talk about miraculous cures they can't explain. But if a little girl has an arm cut off and it is not possible to sew it back on, then she won't grow another one, no matter how much everyone prays for her. And if Keisha was born with a brain that doesn't work right, then I think it is going to stay that way. We need to get focused on how we all can live with her disability, and on getting Keisha the training she needs to have as good a life as possible. We need to stop chasing what is never going to happen." He then turned over and went to sleep.

The words cut deeply. They ripped at Tanya's heart. At some profoundly hidden place in her being, she knew he was right. That was why it hurt so much. Tanya cried for most of a sleepless night. A dam inside her had burst. She had no idea all those tears were still bottled up inside her. By morning she felt hurt, exhausted and washed out. But she was also strangely relieved.

Months later, with the help of friends in a support group for parents of children with mental retardation, Tanya would look back on her months in denial and gain insight into her journey. She learned from the group that denial is often a spontaneous reaction to a painful situation. It is a way of coping with the unthinkable. It can serve the purpose of helping someone continue to deal with the everyday problems of life for a period of time without being overwhelmed by emotional pain.

"While denial is a natural coping mechanism," Tanya's group leader had said, "a person who has cut an artery, and is in denial, could quickly bleed to death. Denial often delays critical early interventions and necessary actions to address very real problems. Delay can add exponentially to the tragedy of an initial event. You only have to think of a wife in denial about her abusive husband, or a teenager in denial about the risks of pregnancy and sexually transmitted disease, in order to understand that denial can cause dangerous delays in necessary actions."

"Denial also consumes tremendous energy," Tanya was told, "because it requires vigilant effort to maintain it. A person in denial may experience being tired most of the time." Tanya remembered her exhaustion during that period of her life. "Such energy usually could be better employed to deal with the real challenges presented by the underlying problem," the leader continued. "But often it is wasted on protecting and preserving a vulnerable self-deception."

Tanya learned from her group leader that there are two levels of denial. Primary denial is a refusal to recognize that a tragic event has occurred and that a problem requiring action exists. Secondary denial, which occurs when the realities of the problem make it impossible to maintain primary denial, admits that a problem exists, but minimizes the serious nature of the situation. In place of the delusions of invincibility that accompany primary denial, secondary denial constructs counterfeit hopes. Bargaining often occurs during secondary denial. In light of these insights, Tanya reflected upon her journey. She was able to see that the pre-school conference had moved her out of primary denial and into secondary denial, that frantic period of searching for a better diagnosis and a miraculous cure.

Tanya also learned about the self-defeating nature of denial.

"The problem with denial, even secondary denial," the group leader had said, "is that emotional healing and constructive action are virtually impossible as long as the reality of a serious problem goes unrecognized and unacknowledged. Denial is insidious because self-deceit is so difficult to recognize. How easily we recognize the denial of others, and how difficult it is to see our own. Denial is seductive because, for a while, it feels so much better than going through what one suspects will be unbearable pain."

The support group helped Tanya focus on learning more about mental retardation and the services that could help her daughter. As a consequence, she became better able to devote her energies to the difficult task of parenting, and to securing the appropriate professional resources and educational programming her daughter needed.

One Sunday, almost a year after her husband had penetrated her defenses with what felt like harsh words at the time, their pastor preached a sermon titled, "Denial is not a River in Egypt." He told about King David and other people in the Bible who tried to live in denial and who needed prophets to get them to face reality. In the sermon, the pastor said, "Everyone knows that an ostrich does not make danger go away by burying its head in the sand. Yet we human beings will go to great lengths to live in denial about our problems and the dangers of our behaviors. It is as though we constantly long for the sense of security and well-being that we once knew in the womb. And because we cannot return to the womb, we construct a second-hand universe. We construct a kind of delusional sphere around ourselves to assure us we are not like other human beings, that we never have serious problems, and that tragic things cannot happen to us. Whenever an event in life puts a crack in that illusion, we work as hard as we can to patch it up. We use just about anything, the psychological and spiritual equivalents of band-aids, bailing wire, and masking tape, until real life makes such frantic efforts no longer possible."

"Denial," the pastor continued, "even if it is expressed as religious hope, is a type of unfaith. It is a refusal to face reality, the reality of God's universe where pain and suffering are a part of life. It is an unwillingness to acknowledge and respond in faith to our own unique tragic experiences, as God, in compassion, intends for us to do. It is a spiritual blindness. It shields us from the emotional pain of viewing tragic reality. But it also blocks us from the spiritual resources available to us as persons of faith during such times."

"Denial is an escape from the life that God has called a person of faith to live. It is a hiding not only from a particularly unpleasant reality, but also from the fullness of creation in which God has placed us. The created universe is filled with a multitude of unpleasant realities. And living in denial is a failure of the spirit to hear and receive God's word that in all things God's grace is sufficient."

It was an important moment of clarity for Tanya. Just as the people in Biblical days needed prophets to break through their denial, she knew that she had needed others to break through her illusions. The pastor had pointed out that when people's lives are addressed by prophets in times of denial, they can be traumatic experiences. Tanya remembered the first time she had learned of Keisha's retardation, and how angry it had made her. When the pre-school director broke through her primary denial, Tanya was tempted to find a different pre-school and start over. And Tanya was more angry and hurt with her husband, the night he penetrated her secondary denial, than she ever had been before. She stayed angry with him for days. She fantasized about things she could say to hurt him as badly as he had hurt her. But she could not go back to the way it was before. She no longer could patch up her illusion. For better or worse, she now had to come to terms with the reality and permanence of Keisha's disability.

As the preacher concluded his sermon that morning, he said something that gave Tanya a whole new perspective on her experience. "It is the grace of God," the minister said, "that allows us to face our sufferings realistically, to accept them and to deal with them constructively." For Tanya, the agents of that grace were those who dared to penetrate her denial. In doing so, they became God's instruments as they opened up new possibilities for the future, both for her and her daughter.

The pastor also had a word that morning for those who had not yet faced a serious tragedy in their lives. "Spiritual preparation before tragedy strikes sometimes can mean that external intervention is unnecessary. A person of faith can pray for the insight and honesty to recognize the temptation to live in denial when tragedy comes, and the courage to resist its seduction. And a person of faith also can pray for the assurance that denial is unnecessary, because absolutely nothing is so terrible that it cannot be faced with God's comfort, support and guidance. Let us remember the words of the Apostle Paul:

> 'Praise be to the God and Father of our Lord Jesus Christ, the Father of compassion and the God of all comfort, who comforts us in all our troubles, so that we can comfort those in any trouble with the comfort we ourselves have received from God.' " (2 Cor. 1:3-4 NIV)

"And what if our spiritual preparation is inadequate for the magnitude of the tragedy? What if, despite our efforts to avoid it, we slip into denial? Faith requires us to recognize that when the smashing of our illusions comes, through whatever agents, it is the compassionate activity of God. God is calling us back to reality and to God's comforting care. And it will surely come, for God will not forsake us in our time of need. The only question is, 'What will we do when that time comes?' "

"What indeed!" Tanya said beneath her breath. She was glad she had found a support group made up of people who had been through their own times of denial. She knew she probably had gotten through her own denial much more quickly than she would have without them. And she was amazed at the relief she felt at not having to shore up her self-deceptions any longer.

Chapter 3:
You Can Run But You Will
Only Get Tired

"Where can I go from your Spirit?
Where can I flee from your presence?
If I go up to the heavens, you are there;
If I make my bed in the depths, you are there."
(Psalm 139:7-8 NIV)

Escape

When most of God's creatures experience danger, they choose either *fight* or *flight* as a survival strategy. Human beings are no exception. When faced with a threat, we generally choose either to struggle with the challenge, or we attempt to escape it. Who among us, when we have perceived a perilous situation, has not experienced an aggressive impulse, or the urge to run away?

Society tends to associate *fight* with courage and *flight* with cowardice. But in reality *fight* also can be a foolish response, and *flight* a wise one. The best generals know how to advance their armies when conditions are favorable and how to retreat if necessary in order to fight another day.

A Natural Response

When we are in great emotional pain, the impulse to flee is a natural response. Just as denial can be a short-term strategy that protects, a temporary escape can be beneficial, as well. It offers respite from emotional exhaustion and postpones the torturous work of dealing with the overwhelming practical problems that come with a great loss. Sometimes the wisest thing a grieving person can do is to go to another place for a while, whether geographically or mentally.

On the other hand, clearly there are times when running from our situations only makes them worse. That is particularly true when our difficulties have been caused by our own selfish and irresponsible behaviors. The narrative about Adam and Eve hiding from God in the garden after their disobedience is the story of every child that ever has disobeyed a parent and tried to avoid the consequences. Most of us agree that when children are not held accountable, they seldom grow up to be responsible members of society. And when adults attempt to escape responsibility for their harmful actions, they often compound the suffering of others while continuing down a slippery slope of their own making.

But what about the desire to run away when faced with tragic circumstances not of our own making? *When we suffer such personal tragedies, there is nothing wrong with feeling the desire to escape. In the face of emotional suffering, such feelings are legitimate human emotions. Depending on the conditions, neither is there anything intrinsically wrong with actually taking a break from the intensity of one's grief.* Such respite can be helpful to the healing process.

DANGEROUS ROUTES

Escape in the midst of grief can take many forms. *Not all escape routes lead to healing.* Some of the paths we may choose in order to flee from our emotional pain can lead to increased suffering. That is primarily because some types of running away are self-destructive and have the potential to bring great harm to others.

One of the more common strategies for escape is some form of *sensuality.* We have seen how the numbness of shock can be perpetuated chemically by continuing the use of tranquilizers and painkillers long after the initial shock has passed. The use of alcoholic beverages to reduce one's pain also can lead to alcohol abuse and addiction.

Overeating is another typical strategy. The initial shock of a personal loss frequently destroys the desire to eat. But when the shock begins to ease, many of us turn to comfort foods in order to reduce our sense of pain. Consequently, it is not unusual for some of us to gain a considerable amount of weight following a personal loss.

We would be remiss also if we did not mention the potential to escape into sexual activity. The loneliness and insecurity we experience at a time of grief can be overwhelming. If we have lost a spouse to divorce or death, we soon may find ourselves, as the country song suggests, "looking for love in all the wrong places."

Other forms of sensual escape can be as seemingly benign as going on a shopping binge, watching a great deal of television, playing video games for hours on end, or indulging in excessive sleep. But any type of sensuality carries great risks and can delay the healing process indefinitely.

TEMPORARY RETREATS

Nevertheless, an appropriate type of retreat often can be as important to a person's successful negotiation of the journey of grief as is facing the tragedy and struggling to deal with its implications. *Whether fight or flight is the right strategy depends on time and circumstance.* This point is well illustrated in Biblical narratives. When Moses killed the Egyptian slave master he fled to the land of Midian. After a long time, God spoke to Moses from a burning bush and Moses returned to Egypt where he repeatedly *challenged* Pharaoh to let the Hebrew people go. Elijah the prophet *confronted and defeated* the priests of Baal in a life-and-death contest on Mount Carmel. But when Jezebel threatened to murder him, Elijah *fled* into the desert and to a cave on Mount Horeb. Then, when God spoke to the prophet in a "gentle whisper," Elijah was sent back to face his enemies once again.

It is important to note that in both stories it is clear it was God who led these prophets to their places of retreat and God who cared for them there. And it is God who, in God's time, called these prophets to return and to face their enemies.

From a faith perspective, there are times when God knows we need to flee from the trials and tribulations of the world to our own versions of a desert retreat. Such a place could be the home of relatives or friends where we feel safe, and where others can help care for our needs. Perhaps we have a special vacation place, such as in the mountains, on a lake, or at a beach where past experiences tell us, if we spend some time there, we can expect to regain our spiritual serenity. Or maybe there is a place in our imagination, possibly a scene we remember from our childhood, or a setting we have wished for in our hearts. When we close our eyes, each of us has the capacity to visit our own special places and to find calm for our stormy souls.

But whether our retreat is geographical or mental, the time inevitably comes when it is no longer a good thing for us to remain in our places of refuge. There is no such thing as a long-term geographical cure for grief, because we take our heartaches with us wherever we go. And mental journeys cannot be sustained for long, because the realities of our everyday lives and the hurt within us intrude and demand attention.

Retreats are intended to be temporary respites. They can help us to prepare for the difficulties we must face. In times of tragedy, they can help begin the healing process, but they cannot complete it. For that to happen, we must face our losses and allow God to lead us through the dark valley of our grief.

That is why God calls us to return, and to confront head on the reasons for our withdrawal. *If we listen, God speaks to us when our season of respite is over, and God assures us that God will be with us to help us in our struggles.*

It is, of course, a common experience to want to stay in a place of refuge indefinitely. As the disciple Peter wanted to remain on the mountain top of the Transfiguration, but was required to come down and face his time of trial, we also desire to remain in retreat for as long as possible, but are called, instead, to return to the real world and to face our difficulties.

In times of loss and emotional pain, it is important to seek God's guidance. If we try to run away when we are supposed to stay and face our time of trial, or if we choose a method of escape which is potentially self-destructive, we soon will discover that our troubles follow us and multiply. If we retreat in order to prepare for what is to come, but overstay the time of our return, we can seriously delay, and even prevent, the long-term healing we need. In either case we are choosing to live in unfaith. But *if we are able to trust that God's love is with us in our time of grief, and that God's Spirit will provide comfort and guidance sufficient to our needs, then we will be free to make the decisions and to take the actions necessary for the successful negotiation of our journey.*

Wayne

Wayne was a successful graphic artist. His wife was expecting a child, and the two of them recently had purchased a new home in order to accommodate their growing family. Then one Monday, as Wayne reported for work, he was surprised to be told his company was downsizing and that he was no longer employed. Before mid-morning he had packed up his personal things, said goodbye to the friends he had worked with for six years, and returned home.

At first he was confident he would be able to find another job quickly. But after a few weeks of making calls and submitting applications, he became discouraged. He was a highly skilled graphic artist. But there were no openings anywhere. Soon his wife, Jeanie, who had not worked outside their home for years, had gone back to work as a minimum wage temporary office assistant. Despite her contribution to the family finances, the bills were piling up, with no light visible at the end of the tunnel.

When it actually sank in that being terminated had destroyed his sense of security and had shattered his dreams for the future, Wayne began to feel hopeless. Such dark and negative feelings were extremely uncomfortable. He was a man who previously had been known for his cheerful demeanor. He hated the way he felt. He wanted to feel good again.

There had been a time when Wayne had dealt with unpleasant emotions by turning to alcohol. But that had been years before. With the help of AA, Wayne had gotten sober and had stayed that way for more than ten years. Only a few months after joining AA, he and Jeanie had dedicated their lives to Christ and joined a church. After a few more months, he had dropped out of AA. Because he was active in church and trying to live a Christian life, he considered his drinking days to be far behind him. In the midst of the shock over his job loss and financial problems, the thought of having a beer occurred to him, but he managed to put it out of his mind.

Soon, however, Wayne found another way to deal with his personal pain. He always had wanted a large truck with off-road capability, and one day he decided having one might alleviate his unhappiness. While Jeanie was at work, and without discussing it with her, he traded his old car for the truck of his dreams. The payments were more than twice those for the car. A few weeks later he backed a top-of-the-line bass boat, which he also had managed to buy on credit, into the garage.

How he had been able to get credit without a job was a mystery to Jeanie. Their credit had been reasonably good before the job loss. They owned a home, and they had kept their bills and credit cards almost current by making at least minimum payments. But because his credit was now marginal, the interest rates on Wayne's new major purchases were exorbitant. He was upside-down on the truck and boat before he had made a single payment. Furthermore, new card offers came in the mail each day, and after being laid off, Wayne had applied for some of them. It felt like free money to him. If they were dumb enough to offer him credit, he was not about to refuse it. He could use the money.

The mail also was filled with bills. Each day Wayne would throw the unopened bills and past due notices into a desk drawer. For a while, that kept them out of sight and out of mind. Sometimes, when he needed spending money, he would write a check. The checks began to bounce, and Wayne was hit with bad check fees from both the banks and the stores where he had written them.

When Jeanie realized what was happening, she was filled with panic. The couple argued. Wayne stormed out and went fishing. Jeanie desperately attempted to contact the stores and banks, to pick up the checks, to pay the fees and repair the damage as best she could. But there was not enough money, and their ability to pay by check now had been ruined.

After buying the truck and boat, Wayne spent most of his days fishing at the local reservoir. He only consciously thought about his financial problems when he returned home in the evening. It was difficult not to think about them, because the bill collectors were calling continuously. Wayne made promises to them he knew he could not keep, just to end the annoyance, albeit temporarily. The couple's credit went from bad to disastrous. Within a few months, both his new boat and truck had been repossessed. His fishing days were ended.

It was not long after the repossessions that Wayne began to sleep late. When he got up, he did not bother to shave. For most of the day he would sit in his family room with the shades drawn, watching television. His wife, Jeanie, came home each day to a kitchen filled with dirty dishes, and to unmade beds and a cluttered house. She had been tolerant at first, but she soon began to feel resentment. One day, when she walked through the door and saw Wayne asleep on the couch with trash all around him, she exploded. They argued heatedly. Wayne walked out, got in Jeanie's car, and drove off. He did not return until four in the morning. He tried to slip into the bedroom unnoticed. Jeannie could smell the alcohol before he reached the bed.

From that day forward, whenever Jeanie would come home, she would find Wayne surrounded by beer cans. Soon after Jeanie arrived each day, Wayne would leave and not return until the early morning. Some nights Jeanie was highly suspicious she smelled women's perfume along with the smell of alcohol. The two of them could not talk any more without arguing. Jeanie now was terrified. Wayne was terrified too, and it was taking more and more booze to bury his feelings of impending doom.

In desperation, Jeanie woke Wayne up late one Sunday morning and told him she was planning to leave him. That got Wayne's attention. They spent the day talking about all their difficulties. In the end, Jeanie agreed to give Wayne a chance to save their marriage. And Wayne agreed to take some serious action. The first thing he did was to call his old AA sponsor, Hal.

Wayne and Hal met at a local diner for a cup of coffee that same evening. "You look terrible," Hal said, "What's going on?"

Wayne described how he had been laid off, the spending, the repossessions, the tension with Jeanie, the boozing and the one-night stands. "It's such a mess. I've dug a deep hole for myself, and I don't think there is any way to climb out."

Hal listened patiently to Wayne's story, before responding. "First things first," the sponsor said. "Do you want to get well?"

Wayne was not surprised by the question, though it hurt him deeply. Hal had asked him the same one a long time ago when they first met at a Friday night meeting. Wayne also recognized it as a question Jesus once asked a paralyzed man, according to the Gospel of John. Wayne sensed where Hal was going with it. "Of course I do, I wouldn't be here if I didn't," Wayne replied in an irritated tone. "But I don't know where to start."

"If you want to get well," Hal said, "you can't lie around waiting for someone to rescue you from your own folly. You wouldn't be in this condition if you simply had taken the action that was necessary when you first lost your job, instead of running away and hiding from your troubles. Think about it. How has running from your troubles worked for you?"

"Terrible." Wayne readily admitted.

"That's right," Hal responded. "If you had done then what you needed to do, you wouldn't have nearly the troubles you have now. But this is not the time to worry about that. There is nothing to be gained by wringing your hands over should of and might have, or by punishing yourself with self-blame. If you want things to be better, the first thing you have to do is to get out of the booze. And if you're going to get out of the booze, you're going to have to go with me to a meeting tonight, pick up a white chip, and make ninety meetings in ninety days. That's the only way I'm going to work with you again. There are a lot of things you can do after you get out of the booze, but the first thing you have to do is stop running from your troubles. And right now that means get sober. You aren't even able to think clearly right now, because your addiction is thinking for you."

Wayne did go with Hal to a meeting that night. He committed himself to abstinence by picking up a white poker chip. He also went to ninety more meetings over the next ninety days. Wayne also rode with Hal to a regional conference where a series of guest speakers with strong programs of recovery were scheduled to present.

At the conference, one of the guest speakers identified himself as a person of faith, who nevertheless had become an alcoholic. "Persons of faith," he said, "do not have immunity from the desire to run from reality. And there are many ways to run. Some people try to buy their way out of difficulties. For many, the pleasure they get from buying things is a favorite escape from the negative realities of life. Some persons are more inclined to abuse prescription drugs in order to avoid their emotional pain, often doctor shopping in order to assure a continuing supply. Others try to escape their feelings by turning to food, finding comfort in continuous grazing on snacks and late night visits to ice cream containers in the freezer. At the other extreme, there are those who diet and exercise, obsessively preoccupied with the notion that the thinner they get, the happier they will be. Still others bury themselves in television programs that let them live vicariously through fictional characters and celebrities who appear to have better lives than their own. For me, it was alcohol."

"I also know persons of faith," the speaker continued, "who try to deal with their suffering by embracing some form of religious fanaticism. They develop a preoccupation and obsession with a particular religious leader, or with a new belief system. They expend great energies in attempting to convert others to their newly found ways. In my opinion such fanaticism never should be confused with spiritual growth and authentic faith. It is not about a deepening relationship with God or a growing empathy with others who suffer. It is not about finding spiritual serenity in the midst of the troubles of life. Rather, it is a frantic attempt to construct an illusion of certainty in a world of insecurity. It is about the desperation to find protection from life's realities and about defending that notion fiercely. It is not about running to God in time of trouble, but about running away from God in order to hide behind a religious tree."

"It is important to understand that any form of running from reality is, in reality, a running away from God. The problem with running from our troubles is that when we do so we just make matters worse. When we run, we waste vital energies and resources that we need in order to deal constructively with the crisis in our lives. And we soon learn that *we can run, but not only can we not hide, we will only get tired*. The first step toward recovery for anyone who runs from their troubles is to recognize and admit the futility and self-destructiveness of not facing reality. "

"The second step," the speaker went on to say, "is to seek help from others and from God. The only thing truly required of a person of faith who is running away from emotional pain, is to turn around and go get help. The chief reason we run from things in our lives is we have the mistaken notion that we must face them alone, and we are overwhelmed by that prospect. Few of us are strong enough to face real difficulties alone. The good news is we don't have to."

"Some of us," the speaker said, "are rich in those who love and care about us, and some of us are poor. But even those who feel that nobody cares are wrong. You may not yet know them, but persons who care about you are there, nevertheless. There are people in this room who care about you more than you possibly could imagine. The world has an abundance of caring, compassionate people who want to help those who are truly in need and are sincere in their desire to overcome their difficulties. Some people who need help know exactly where to go."

Wayne thought about his friend and sponsor, Hal.

"Others may have to search in new places," the speaker continued. "But compassionate help is available. Fortunately, there are support groups made up of others with similar problems to yours, no matter what your problem is. And there are organizations, professional counselors and kind pastors who also are there for those who can set their pride aside long enough to seek help."

"It is ironic that we tend to run from God when we need God the most. It is an even greater irony that God loves us and desires that we turn to our loving Creator in times of trouble. The good news is that there is no place to go that God has not gone before us. There is no place we can run to that is so far away that God is not already there, and waiting to give us aid, if only we become willing to ask for help. When we are tempted to run from the pain of our difficulties, that is when we need to recognize that by fleeing we make things far worse for ourselves and for others. It is a season to pray for strength, for serenity and for guidance."

The speaker that day, Wayne thought, was the best he ever had heard. He purchased a recording of the speaker's message, and listened to it again and again.

Once he had some sobriety under his belt and was experiencing some spiritual centeredness, Wayne was able to take some other actions to begin to address his problems. With the help of Hal, Wayne decided it was time to come to terms with the fact he was not going to get another graphic artist job in the area. It was time to look for some other kind of work. After putting in many applications, he was hired as a management trainee in a fast food restaurant. It was not the kind of work he would have liked, and it did not pay nearly as well as his old job. But it was work, and it finally provided some much-needed additional income. He and Jeanie visited a financial counselor. With her help, the couple was able to develop a budget and a plan for dealing with their debts.

Almost a year after that initial meeting with Hal, Wayne himself was asked to speak at an AA meeting. As he shared his story, Wayne told the group he had learned something new and life-changing from his troubles. "When I lost my job, I thought God had abandoned me. I was wrong. It was I who abandoned God. Like the prodigal son in the Bible, I was the one who ran away from my Heavenly Father, my Higher Power, to another life, and squandered all the blessings I had received. God had given me a new reality, the reality of a lost job. I abandoned God when I refused to face the reality that God had given me. I ran away from God because I didn't want to face that reality. I wanted another reality. So I turned again to alcohol and to every other temporary pleasure I could find."

"But God didn't give up on me. God gave me a wonderful wife who would not put up with my foolishness. God gave me a great sponsor who does not let me get away with anything other than rigorous honesty with myself and with others. My Higher Power has given me the beginnings of a new recovery and a new experience of His spiritual presence in my life. I still have terrible credit. I continue to have financial difficulties. But with God's help, I am facing my difficulties. One day at a time, things are getting better."

"I have found it is never too late to trust that God will hear our prayers and come to our aid," Wayne said. "One day at a time, I am trying to live in reality and to live in trust, for I believe God keeps promises and,

'God is our refuge and strength,
an ever present help in trouble.'"
(Psalm 46:1 NIV)

"In conclusion, let me leave you with this question. Is there some reality that you are unwilling to face today?

Chapter 4:
Where is a Superhero
When You Really Need One?

"Three times I pleaded with the Lord to take it away from me. But he said to me, 'My grace is sufficient for you, for my power is made perfect in weakness.'"
(2 Cor 12:8-9 NIV)

Victimism

When we learn on the evening news about a terrible event, such as a deadly tornado that has plowed through a residential community, we often describe the dead, the wounded, and those who have lost loved ones and valuable property, as *victims*. Such a term seems appropriate because the individuals touched by those events did not have the ability to prevent them from happening.

When we are not responsible for our own suffering, understanding ourselves as victims may be beneficial. It is unrealistic and unhealthy to assume we have the power to protect ourselves, and those we love, from *all* harm. And it is self-defeating to assume blame for circumstances beyond our control. When we do, we compound the already overwhelming burdens of our losses.

While it may be helpful at times to think of ourselves as victims, it also can be detrimental. As we have seen in preceding chapters on denial and escape, getting stuck in a particular grief reaction can postpone and even prevent healing. Victimism is no exception. If we are struggling with feelings of powerlessness and guilt, a long-term victim role may be especially seductive.

POWERLESSNESS

When we become victims of some terrible event beyond our control, we usually have an overwhelming sense of powerlessness. Most of us like to think that we are in control of the circumstances of our lives, and that if we are smart enough and do all the right things, nothing bad can happen. We may know better, in our hearts. We may witness the innocent suffering of others. Yet we may remain confident that such things will not happen to us. When they do, the illusion of our ability to control our lives, particularly with regard to our security, is shattered.

Powerlessness is not a pleasant sensation. We feel defeated and sapped of our strength. We question our own abilities, and find it difficult to trust others. When, for example, a woman has been the victim of a violent crime, such as rape, she often is filled with the terror which comes with feeling vulnerable and defenseless despite any safety measures she might take. She may add locks to her doors and windows, install a security system, and stay awake at night. But every protective action she employs serves to underscore her sense of being robbed of power over her own body and her own life.

But just as it is a fantasy that we are able to secure our lives against all potential harm, it also is an illusion to believe that any outside force or event can rob us permanently of our God-given dignity and inner freedom. People in the most limiting and terrible of circumstances often demonstrate this truth. We may know of someone, for example, who has been paralyzed from the neck down, powerless to do anything for himself, who chooses not to be angry or bitter, but to be grateful for daily blessings and to respond to his caretakers with a gentle spirit. And no one has demonstrated this freedom more clearly than Jesus, who, while he was dying a cruel and painful death on the cross, forgave those who were victimizing him.

The sense of powerlessness can be debilitating if we succumb to it. But it has the potential for healing, if it reminds us that life comes to each of us both as things we can control and as things we cannot. *During times of personal grief, it is important to focus on the things that we can do.* The emotion of powerlessness reminds us that we are human beings, and not God. Yet it also represents an opportunity to realize that God has given each of us the freedom to decide the way in which we will relate to our situations. As long as we have consciousness, the power of that freedom will never be taken from us. And under most conditions, there are practical actions that can and should be taken as well.

GUILT

Guilt is another emotion many of us have when we become victims of tragedy. When we experience a personal tragedy, we are prone to ask ourselves very early in the grieving process whether what happened was our fault, or whether we might have been able to do something which would have prevented it. Even when we cannot think of anything we could have done to change the outcome, we still may have a general sense of guilt. *We may be reluctant to think of ourselves as innocent victims, even when reason tells us that we bear no responsibility for what has occurred.*

Sometimes those who have survived a tragedy, when others have not, develop what the psychologists call *survivors' guilt.* They feel guilty not because they believe they were responsible for causing the tragedy. They feel guilty because they survived it and others did not. They do not feel they deserved to survive any more than those who were less fortunate.

In addition to survivors, misplaced guilt is often seen in those who are victims of violent crimes. We also are likely to experience it if a loved one has become an addict, or committed suicide. And we probably will be burdened with these unwarranted feelings if a relative has murdered, or carried out some other atrocious deed.

In these and similar cases, progress toward recovery and healing can be delayed for a very long time. If we are consumed with torturing ourselves with *what-ifs*, with accusations, and with self-blame, we become emotionally and spiritually paralyzed in the face of our difficulties.

When we struggle with feelings of guilt while we are in fact not guilty of anything relevant, we waste the energy we need for dealing with the legitimate work of negotiating the journey of grief. Even when, in hindsight, we think of something we might have done if only we could have anticipated the outcome, guilt is unproductive, except perhaps to motivate us and guide us when facing future situations.

But what if we do bear some responsibility for a tragic situation? What if our careless or selfish decisions have resulted in our suffering or the innocent suffering of others? *Just as it is detrimental to feel guilty about things truly beyond our control, it is also unhealthy to avoid accountability for those things for which we are responsible.*

When we truly are guilty we may choose to play the victim role instead of admitting our wrongs. If we refuse to acknowledge our legitimate guilt, we are unable to undergo the changes necessary for healing. And as long as we fail to accept responsibility for our actions, we are likely to repeat similar behavior in the future and to cause additional suffering.

For persons of faith, healthy grieving involves sorting out our personal transgressions from uncontrollable circumstances. And if we bear responsibility for harm to ourselves, or to others, it means we must honestly confess our sins and ask God, in faith, for forgiveness. We must pray for the willingness to receive God's mercy, and for the courage to seek forgiveness from everyone we have harmed.

If we are able to be honest with ourselves, with God, and with those we have wronged, and if we humbly ask for forgiveness, there is nothing we have done that is so terrible that it cannot be forgiven. Of course, it is likely there will be times when other people will be unwilling to forgive us. But that is not our responsibility. If we are genuine in our repentance, we can be assured God *will* forgive us. And experiencing God's forgiveness is the prerequisite for moving on, for making amends, for righting wrongs, and for taking the next steps toward healing.

THE HERO WITHIN

When we choose to live as victims we do not look within for solutions. The difficult spiritual work, which is our share of the healing process, is left undone, since we constantly are looking outwardly for some type of rescue. This may be in the form of an expectation that some new event will happen to us, such as winning the lottery, or that some person will appear to take us away from it all, or to make everything OK again. We wait and hope that such a rescue will take place.

As people of faith, we often pray for God to take away our difficulties. Many of us have experienced, at one time or another, that our prayers, whether for ourselves or for others, have been heard and answered. But what are we to conclude when people of faith experience outcomes different from those for which they have prayed? For example, an entire church earnestly prays for a child injured in an automobile accident. She remains in a coma and eventually dies. A family surrounds the bed of a seriously ill man praying through the night for his recovery. He does not make it. Such things happen every day.

When their prayers are not answered according to their desires, it is not unusual for misguided people of faith to blame their own weakness of faith. Unfortunately, they have failed to understand the difference between those things that are up to God and the things for which we are responsible. And they have failed to grasp that all prayers need to be offered in the spirit of Jesus' words in the Garden of Gethsemane "Yet not my will, but yours be done."

When we are in the midst of the journey of grief, we do need rescuing, but not necessarily as we would like. Sometimes help comes in strange forms. It may be an accidental meeting or conversation. Other people sometimes can be the instrument of the necessary *Word*, even when they are not consciously aware of that role. So can the movies and television programs we watch, or the books we read. From a faith perspective, such encounters are no accidents. *God constantly is trying to speak to us and will use any means necessary to get our attention and to help us to negotiate our journeys safely and successfully.*

That *Word*, when it comes to us, may be asking us to die to the illusion that we will be rescued from the consequences of our personal losses through outside intervention. *God may be calling us to look within, and to find, with God's help, that hero whom God has created within us when we were made in God's image.* No matter how much that spiritual reality has been damaged by unfaith, and that hero suppressed by victimism, God can awaken and restore it. If we freely surrender our lives to the care, guidance and strength of God, and allow the hero within to be released, *we will be no longer victims, but victors.* Nothing about our situation may be changed, but everything will be transformed.

ANDREW

Mr. Jim and Ms. Jenny moved into the house next door to Andrew a little before the boy's eighth birthday. Andrew had been disappointed at first. He had hoped his new neighbors would be a family with children near his own age. What he got instead was a gray-haired retired couple.

Andrew was lonely. His mother would take him to soccer. But she was too busy with Beth, his baby sister, to play with him. His dad's job required a lot of traveling. It seemed to Andrew that his father was almost always away. And when he was home, he was too tired to do anything with his son. The boys and girls Andrew knew from school and church lived in other neighborhoods. Without friends nearby, and with a sister who was still in diapers, the boy had to entertain himself most of the time.

Much of Andrew's playtime was centered on his preoccupation with superheroes. He had a collection of superhero action figures and costumes decorating his bedroom and littering the house. He owned all of the Superman, Batman and Spiderman movies and watched them so often that he knew much of the dialogue by heart. He not only dressed up in a new superhero costume every Halloween, but he could be seen playing in his back yard most Saturdays wearing one of the colorful outfits. Mr. Jim and Ms. Jenny often watched, as they sat on their porch, while Andrew leapt off of the ledge of his jungle gym and chased the bad guys through the tunnel and under the slide.

It did not take long for Andrew to change the way he felt about his new neighbors. Ms. Jenny baked cookies and bought treats for Andrew and his little sister, mostly around holidays, but sometimes for no reason at all. Mr. Jim worked outside for a little while most days, tending his flowers. Andrew, who came to watch at first, soon found himself helping pull weeds and push the wheelbarrow. Mr. Jim was a kind gentleman, and most afternoons Andrew spent some time sitting on the porch rocking and talking with him. With a little encouragement from his new friend, Andrew would talk about school, and soccer, and most important of all, superheroes. Mr. Jim always was interested in these subjects. On a really good day, their discussions would lead to one of the old man's stories. Andrew loved Mr. Jim's stories.

When Andrew was eleven, his Mom and Dad began to fight a lot. Mr. Jim and Ms. Jenny knew there was trouble next door. They sometimes could hear the yelling and slamming of doors. At first Andrew did not mention the family problems to Mr. Jim, and though the old gentleman could see the distress on the young boy's face, he did not pry. They talked on the porch each afternoon as if nothing had changed. That lasted until Andrew's twelfth birthday party.

Although the birthday fell on a Monday, the party was planned for a Saturday evening. All of Andrew's aunts, uncles, and cousins were invited. So were three other families who were friends of the parents. Two of Andrew's cousins were boys, and the other guests each brought a son. All were near Andrew's age. Andrew's cup of excitement was running over. Laughing and shouting, the boys chased each other around the back yard and the yards of the nearest neighbors. They played some soccer, and soldiers, and tag. Everyone ate the tasty catered meal, and Andrew got to open his presents. One of them was a video game, and all five boys were soon sitting in front of a screen, mesmerized by the action.

At first, because of the noise from the game, the children did not notice the grownups making some noise of their own. What happened next might not have occurred, if it had not been for all the beer consumed earlier in the day by the parents. An argument broke out between Andrew's mother and the mother of one of the other boys. There was angry screaming and the crashing and tinkling of broken glass. At first Andrew and his playmates could not understand what was being said. But when they paused their game, they heard very clearly. Andrew's mom was accusing one of the other boy's moms of having an affair with Andrew's father. Within minutes, all the visitors retrieved their children and left.

That night, Andrew's parents continued to yell at each other for what seemed like several hours. Each of them, without regard to the ears of the children, accused the other of unspeakable infidelities. Sometime that night, after the children were in bed, Andrew's father packed a bag and left. He would never return.

It was a night that changed Andrew's life. His father rented his own apartment, and the woman his mother had argued with at the birthday party left her family within days and moved in with him.

For as long as Andrew could remember, his father had been gone more than he had been home. Now he was gone all the time. He no longer called or came by. Andrew tried to spend the weekend with him once, but it was clear his father and his father's girlfriend did not want him there. Andrew did not like the woman, and he hated all the drinking and smoking. He begged his mother not to make him go back. And she didn't.

It was not long until Andrew's mother had a houseguest of her own. It was someone she brought home one night after a date. The man stayed that night and never left. In a few short weeks, Andrew's universe had been turned upside down, and he was seriously depressed. As soon as his parents had started fighting, Andrew began to pray nightly for God to make them stop. They didn't. When his father left, Andrew prayed for his father to come home and for his parents to reconcile. They didn't.

Soon after the birthday party, Andrew began to talk with Mr. Jim about what was happening to the family. Mr. Jim listened quietly and sympathetically. Andrew felt it was good to have someone to tell his troubles to. One day Andrew broke a long silence as they sat rocking on the porch, by saying, "I thought God was supposed to answer prayers. He sure didn't answer mine."

"You think God isn't answering your prayers?" Mr. Jim asked softly.

"I have prayed over and over for God to make my mom and dad love each other again, and to get back together. It's like God doesn't hear me or care. I think maybe this stuff about God is like the Santa Clause thing," Andrew said with a frown. "Maybe it's just a story grown-ups make up. Maybe there isn't a God, and that's why He doesn't answer my prayers."

"Well, Andrew," Mr. Jim said, "I see you have started asking some of the really tough questions. Do you think it is possible God does answer our prayers, but that He doesn't always answer them the way we want him to?"

"What do you mean?"

"Well, take that Santa Clause thing you mentioned. Can you remember a time when you didn't get what you asked Santa Clause to bring?"

"I don't think so."

"Why do you think that is? Do you think maybe your Mom and Dad made sure you didn't ask Santa for something they couldn't afford or something they didn't want you to have because it would not be good for you?"

"I guess so."

"The Santa thing may have been a made-up story," Mr. Jim continued, "but your mother and father were real. So was their love for you, no matter what it may feel like now. They always wanted you to have a happy Christmas, and didn't want you to be disappointed. But they also did not want you to have a present that would be dangerous or not good for you. You were too young to know what was best for you, so they made sure you got only things that were OK for you to have. I bet there were a lot of other times that you wanted to buy something, or to do something and they said 'No'. Am I right?"

"Oh, Yeah! They said no a lot of times."

"So, do you think they were being just mean?"

After a thoughtful moment, Andrew answered, "No, I think they were trying to be good parents. But what I don't understand is, if they really love me, why is my Mom living with someone besides my Dad, and why did my Dad have to leave? And if he still loves me, then why doesn't he call, or come and take me some place fun, like he used to?"

"I don't know either, Andrew. I think that is wrong of him and the whole thing is a mess. But here's what I believe. I believe God isn't going to make your parents do the right thing, no matter how much you pray for it. God doesn't work like that. God gives people the power of choice, and doesn't take that away even when their choices are bad. I also believe, whether your father really loves you or not, that God loves you and wants what is best for you. And I believe God can still love and take care of each of us in His own way, even when it feels like we are getting a bad deal."

Mr. Jim let Andrew think about this for a moment and then continued. "I believe God wants us to have a good life, the one that God created each of us to have. And I believe only God knows what is best for us. God is even better at that than our parents. And somehow, God will make sure, if we trust God, that what we get in this life are the blessings that God wants us to have. They may not be the particular blessings we asked for, and sometimes they may not look like blessings at first, but they will be exactly what we need."

"But don't you think God wants my Mom and Dad to get back together?"

"That's a tough one. I honestly don't know. But I wonder at this point if the relationship between your parents is not so broken, that, if they did get back together, it would be worse for everyone than the way it is now. I know one thing. It is really tough to live in a house with parents who don't love each other any more, and who even have come to despise one another. But I also know that having your father abandon you is probably the most painful thing a young man can experience."

A week later, Mr. Jim and the boy sat rocking silently on the porch watching a humming bird drink from the flowers in the pots by the steps. "Did I ever tell you about the time my Dad left me?" Mr. Jim asked.

"Your Dad left you?

"It was different from the way your Dad left you," Mr. Jim continued, "but he did leave me. And I don't think I ever quite got over it. It happened back in the Korean War. My Dad was in the Army in World War II, and after the war he joined the Army Reserves.

When the Korean War broke out, they called him back. I was thirteen at the time, and I'll never forget standing at the train station shaking hands with him and telling him goodbye. I tried not to cry, but I didn't quite succeed. The last thing my Dad said to me before he got on the train was, 'You're the man of the house now. You take care of your mother and sister.' I waved to him as the train pulled out of the station. He waved back. It was the last time I ever saw him. He was killed in action a few months later. I really tried to take care of my mom and sister after that, but I'm not sure I did a very good job of it."

"I bet you were really sad when that happened."

"I was. And I had a hard time, just like you are having now, because I prayed so hard for my Dad to be safe and come home, and he never did." After another long silence, Mr. Jim said, "I think I already may have told you that when I was young I used to have a big collection of comic books."

"Yep. And you said almost all of them were about superheroes."

"That's right. And do you know what I did after my Dad was killed? I gathered all of those comic books. I put them in a big empty metal oil drum in my back yard that my parents used to burn trash. And I burned every one of them."

"Why did you do that? Do you know how much money they would be worth today?"

"Probably a lot, Andrew. But I needed to burn them because it was time for me to grow up. I think until my Dad died, I believed in my heart that if I was a good boy, and something really bad was about to happen, some superhero would swoop down and save the day. I think just about everyone wants that. They want a superhero to rescue them from all of life's troubles."

"Don't get me wrong, Andrew. Just about every society that ever has existed has had stories about superheroes. They entertain us. They inspire us to struggle against the evil in this world. They teach us about honesty, justice, courage, and self-sacrifice for the good of others. But the time comes when we need to leave the world of superheroes behind."

"Because they are not real?" Andrew interjected.

"Yes, because they are not real, and because our lives and problems are real, and because we need to face them and deal with them without the fantasy that someone else is going to step in and magically fix our problems."

"But isn't that why we pray? Aren't we asking God to fix our problems?"

"You sure do ask some good questions, Andrew. OK. Here is how I think it works. Sometimes when we ask God to do something, God says 'yes,' and we get what we ask for. There are boys and girls who have prayed for their parents to get back together, and sure enough they did, though not necessarily as soon as the children would have liked. At other times, God says, 'No.' There are many boys and girls who have prayed for their parents to get back together and it did not happen."

"Is that because some kids are good and some are bad?"

"Oh, no! That has nothing to do with it. God loves all of His children and wants them to have good things."

"Then, why does God say no?"

"I think sometimes it is because God doesn't want to break His own rules. Remember, Andrew, when God made people He gave them the freedom to choose, and God does not want to take that away, even when they are doing very bad things. But even when God might be able to answer our prayers without breaking His rules, God sometimes still says 'no.' That is because God is in a better position than you and me to know what good things we need. Sometimes what we ask for is not what we need at all, and sometimes what we don't want is exactly what we need."

"Then, why do we bother to pray?"

"That is another very good question, Andrew. I think God is happy for us to ask for the things we want. But God is not Santa Clause. God is not there to be our magical genie. God is there to strengthen and guide us through the journey of life. Sometimes what we want is for God to make our situation better. But what God wants is for us to grow in our capacity to deal with our troubles, and to grow in faith. So, instead of giving us an improved situation, God offers us the chance to be stronger as a person and in our faith."

"If every time we had a problem, God, like some superhero, magically rescued us, we would remain childish and weak. We would not become the persons God wants us to be. God doesn't want to send us a comic book superhero every time we have a problem. What God wants is for us to work with God to unlock the real hero that he placed within each of us when we were created. Despite whatever we have done, and whatever has happened to us, if we are willing, God can release that hero. And we can face life and all its difficulties with courage, faith, and a loving heart."

"At some point along the way, Andrew," Mr. Jim went on, "the time comes when we must learn how to pray adult prayers. When we grow up in our relationship with God, prayer is no longer about getting God to make our lives be the way we want them to be. It is about having our lives be the way God wants them to be."

"You have a tough situation right now with your Mom and Dad. I wouldn't be surprised if they each married someone else. Maybe soon. You can't do anything about that, Andrew. But what you can do is ask God to help you have the courage and spiritual strength to make the best of that situation. You can ask God to help you get through it, and to use you to help your sister get through it. You can ask God to help you keep on loving your Mom and Dad, and help you to forgive them and the people they have decided to love. You can ask God to help you forgive all of them for whatever they have done that may have been wrong. And you can ask God to help you work on Andrew, to help him to become the person God wants Andrew to be. Now those would be some grown-up prayers."

Andrew thought a lot about that conversation with Mr. Jim over the next few days. He was not ready to burn his collection of superhero movies, costumes and souvenirs, yet. After all, they might be worth a lot of money some day. But he did box them up and put them in the attic. And Andrew did try to ask God to help him the way Mr. Jim had suggested.

The next few years were not smooth sailing for Andrew, by any means. He remained estranged from his father. He didn't always get along with his step-dad. He sometimes got into trouble for not doing what he was supposed to do. But his teen years could have been much worse. With Mr. Jim's encouragement, he joined a church youth group, and in that group he found a kind of second family. With the help of his friends in the group and the church counselors, Andrew grew in his faith and in his desire to know and to do God's will. He was always one of the first ones in the group to volunteer for mission trips and service projects.

When Andrew went off to college, he joined and soon became a leader in the campus Christian movement. During his sophomore year, he was asked to speak at one of the annual Christian rallies for high school age youth, similar to the ones he once had attended with his own youth group.

Looking out on several hundred young people attending the rally that Saturday morning, Andrew told them of the important role Mr. Jim had played in his life after his father and mother had separated and then divorced. "What I wanted at the time was for God to send me a superhero to fix things the way I thought they should be fixed. But as you may have noticed, there never seems to be a superhero around when you really need one."

Andrew noticed nods and smiles in the audience.

"Instead," he continued, "God sent me a real hero in the form of a gray-haired old man who moved into the house next door. We had many talks, sitting on his porch, over the years. He talked to me about life and about God. With a gentle hand, he pointed me to Jesus Christ. Without those talks I know I would have become a very different person."

" One day. when I was fourteen, I saw Mr. Jim sitting on the front porch whittling. I had seen him doing that before. I couldn't believe how good he was at carving animals. One of my prized possessions was a carved mountain lion mounted on a log. Mr. Jim had surprised me a year or so earlier when he had given it to me. That afternoon, I did something I hadn't done before. I went over and asked Mr. Jim if he could teach me to carve an animal. Mr. Jim agreed to teach me, only after he showed me how to work the knife so as not to cut myself."

"Once the safety lesson was done, Mr. Jim said I should start by carving a bear out of a block of wood. 'If you can carve a bear,' he had said, 'you can carve about anything.' So he fetched a block of basswood from his workshop, handed it to me and told me to make a bear.

'But how do I get started. How do I make a bear?' I asked.

'It is real simple' he responded. 'You just take a block of wood and you whittle away everything that is not a bear.'

'You make it sound easy. It can't be that easy,' I protested.

'I didn't say it was easy,' he responded, 'I said it was simple.'

Then he patiently showed me how to outline the bear on the block of wood and I began whittling away everything that was not a bear."

"Mr. Jim is in Heaven, now. He passed away about a year ago. But as I have thought about my journey with him, I have realized how much life is like carving that bear. We show up in life with a lot of potential. That potential can be shaped for good or for evil. God has in mind what God wants us to become, just like I knew I wanted that block of wood to become a bear. Our job, with God's help, is to carve away everything that is not what God wants us to be."

"When my parents separated and got a divorce, I lost being taken care of by my family. And I lost the childish belief that I would never have to face any real problems in life. I know now that God was helping me to grow up, not just as a human being, but also as a Christian. God was helping me leave childhood behind, and was assisting me in carving away everything that was not the person God created me to be. Now let me be clear. God and I are still working on that. I am a work in progress. But one of the things I think has been whittled away, is the child in me, who, when I had a problem, wanted a superhero to come and fix it for me. I no longer sit around and wait for a superhero to come and rescue me from my troubles. I no longer think of God as a kind of heavenly Santa Claus. But with the help of my Heavenly Father, I try to work on my own problems. With God's help, I try to accept the stuff that isn't mine to work on. Together we work on the stuff that we can, and I try to trust God with the rest."

"As I have traveled along my spiritual journey, I have come to realize that I am never alone. Unlike my earthly father, my Heavenly Father never will abandon me. I also have come to know there may not be any superheroes to come and rescue me in this world, but there is a real hero within me. I am not that hero. That hero is a gift from God."

"I believe God placed a hero within each of us when we were created. It says in the Bible that God created us in God's image. The hero that dwells in each of us is a part of the person God has designed, and desires for us to become. I also know from reading the Bible, and from my personal experiences, sin conceals our true nature, and prevents us from realizing God's purpose. But, as people of faith, we know that is not the end of the story."

"I believe Jesus always has lived in my heart. I didn't always know Jesus was there, but he was. And because of a wonderful gray-haired old man, I have come to know Jesus. Through God's amazing grace, I now experience Jesus in my spiritual heart. It is Jesus, the hero within, who strengthens me when I am challenged by life's circumstances. And it is Jesus who whittles at my imperfections and leads me on my journey."

Not long after that speech, Andrew visited Mr. Jim's grave. On the tombstone he placed a beautifully carved bear.

Phase II
The Unwillingness to
Accept Reality

Chapter 5:
Why Do You Keep Asking "Why?"

"My God, my God, why have you forsaken me?
Why are you so far from saving me,
so far from the words of my groaning?"
(Psalm 22:1 NIV)

Questioning

In times of grief, we tend to ask a lot of questions. When we are in shock and denial we ask, "Is this really happening? Is there a way for it not to be true?" When we are trying to avoid facing the reality of our losses through some form of escape, we want to know, "Where can I flee? Where is a safe place?" If we are in the victim role we wonder, "Who is going to rescue me?" "When is it going to happen?"

At some point in our journey of grief, most of us reach the place where it is no longer possible to live in denial, avoidance or false hope. The reality of our situation breaks through our defenses, and we are compelled to face the truth of what has happened, no matter how difficult. To the question whether a personal tragedy is real, we must answer, "Yes." To the question where we can flee to safety, we are forced to answer, "Nowhere." To the questions who or what will come and give us a different situation, and when that will take place, we are required to admit, "It's not going to happen."

At the point when it is no longer possible to avoid facing the reality of our losses and their implications, we often find ourselves uttering a new question. We begin to ask "Why?"

THE WHY? QUESTION

The question *Why?* may be the most asked of all human questions, because we want to believe there is an explanation for everything. Sometimes when we ask *why*, we actually mean *how*, as in questions of *why* things in the physical universe work the way they do. For example, if we ask *why* hurricanes form over the ocean, we probably are expecting a meteorological explanation. On the other hand, when a hurricane strikes our community, causing loss of life and property, the *why* question seldom is about cause and effect. Or if a loved one dies in a car accident and we ask, 'Why?', we usually are not looking for an explanation about someone running a light or passing on a curve. In either case we are seeking something much more profound.

When we ask the question, *why?* in the midst of tragedy, we most often are asking a spiritual question, whether or not we recognize it to be so. *Why?* questions tend to arise when we no longer can avoid facing the reality of our situations, and we long to reach a place on our journey where we again will have some serenity. When we ask *why?* we are expressing a desire to reach acceptance, to make peace with our situations, and to find some spiritual solace. But the question itself is a sign that we are not yet ready to embrace the reality of our losses. Before we can know acceptance, we must continue a while on the journey of grief. We have more work to do.

We all want to believe things happen for a reason in this world. We sometimes imagine that if someone could answer the question 'Why?' to our personal satisfaction, we might be able to make our peace with what has happened. This is particularly true of persons of faith. We may feel we have seen God's mysterious hand working for good in all sorts of situations. But at the moment of being no longer able to avoid coming to terms with our losses, we are unable to see any point to such things. We find ourselves questioning God's justice and love. Such feelings are normal, though we may not feel they are.

While asking *'Why?'* is perfectly natural, the difficulty is that no explanation will satisfy us. If someone says to us, God does not make such things happen, we want to know *why* God made a universe where such stuff happens anyway. If we are counseled that this is a part of God's plan, then we want to know *why,* if God is good, God would make such an awful plan. If someone attempts to explain to us *why* there is evil in the world we ask them *why* innocent victims must suffer for the sins of others. Every explanation results in another question *why.*

WHY ME?

One of the reasons the answers we receive are experienced as inadequate, is that we are asking a profoundly personal question. We are not just asking *why* such things happen *in the universe,* but "Why has this terrible thing happened to *me, or to someone I love?"*

The question *Why me?* arises out of what usually are hidden assumptions about our lives in this world. At some level of our being, we believe bad stuff happens to *other* people. We see it on the news every night. We consider this reality to be regrettable, but to be expected. We may wonder why such awful things happen to innocent people in this world, but rarely do we lose sleep over it. Sometimes particular events may make us especially sad and may create within us a desire to help relieve the suffering of those who have experienced some terrible loss. Yet whether we become involved in their suffering or not is entirely optional.

But it is a different matter when a tragedy impacts us personally. At some level, we think terrible things may happen to *others,* but they are not supposed to happen to *us.* Perhaps this is because, at some dimension of our consciousness, we think of ourselves as special, and therefore as exempt from becoming victims of tragedy. Or maybe it is because we cling to the notion that bad things only happen to bad people, while those who live good lives are supposed to be immune from such things. And if we are persons of faith, we may make the assumption that "a good and faithful servant" will be protected by God at all times from all but the smallest of troubles. So when tragedy strikes us, our cry is not only, "Why is this *happening*?" but, also, "Why is this happening *to me*?"

A SIGN OF ANGUISH

None of this is to say it is wrong for us to ask *why?* questions. Such questions are important components of our journey through grief. For many of us, healing can come only when we have struggled with these questions of the heart. But when we ask them, if we are to continue successfully on our journey, it is important to remember that we seek something deeper than explanations.

When Jesus was dying on the cross, he quoted Psalm 22:1. He cried out to his Heavenly Father, "My God, My God, *why* have you forsaken me?" It should be clear to all thoughtful readers of Scripture, that Jesus was not asking a philosophical question about his suffering. He was expressing to God the Father his anguish, and the feeling of abandonment that we all have when we are alone in our agony. When we remember Jesus on the cross, it is clear we need not be concerned that God is in any way offended by our questioning. Those who ask "*Why?*" can take comfort in the fact that both the writer of the Psalm and Jesus asked the question, during their own most personal tragedies.

Therefore, while the question *"Why me?"* may be for us an indication of a misplaced notion of entitlement in this world, it also should be understood as a cry of the heart. It is a calling out to our Creator to hear our distress. It is a means of letting God know how much pain we are in. Just as children feel the need to let parents know how much they hurt after falling down and scraping their knees, so we too have a mysterious need to express to God the anguish of our emotional pain. And that should be recognized as a clue to the function of the questioning phase in the healing process. When we can be honest with ourselves about the reality of our losses, and when we can be honest with God about the degree of our pain, we are preparing ourselves for healing.

GOD'S QUESTIONS OF US

Much of the book of Job deals with the questions raised by a good and righteous man who experienced unimaginable losses. Job asked God, "Why did I not die in my mother's womb?" "Why have you made me a target?" "Why do you persecute me?" Toward the end of the story, God turned the tables on Job. Up until then, God had listened patiently to Job's lament. But then God commanded Job, "Brace yourself like a man, I will question you, and you shall answer me." What followed was a series of questions designed to make the point that Job, a human being, is not in a position to understand the ways of the Lord of heaven and earth.

When we find ourselves struggling with the questions *"Why?"* and *"Why me?"*, it is helpful for us also to listen for the questions God is asking *us*. God can handle our questioning, just fine. Asking them can help prepare us for the next step of our journey. But we are not likely to take that step successfully, if we do not cease our questioning of God long enough to hear the questions God is asking us.

For example, we may sense that God is asking us, "What attitude are you going to have about your loss?" "Are you going to be bitter and angry?" "Are you going to give in to depression and give up?" "What are you going to do?" Or we may feel ourselves being asked, "When are you going to notice the many ways I am caring for you in your grief?" and "How can this emotionally painful change in your life help you to become a kinder, more loving person?" With such questions, God calls us away from the seduction of self-pity and the temptation to live our lives as a protest against the way life is for all of us.

Cynthia

Cynthia and Mike both believed they were soul mates from the moment they met. That conviction had become even stronger over their twenty-six year marriage. They loved to share experiences, and they cherished every moment when they could be alone together. When their youngest daughter finally went off to college, they celebrated their new opportunity for intimacy and freedom with a second honeymoon on a Caribbean cruise. A few weeks later, forty-eight-year-old Mike dropped dead of a heart attack, while jogging in the park early one Saturday morning. Cynthia felt as if everything that made her life worth living had been destroyed.

Once the initial shock had eased and her denial had worn thin, the forty-seven- year-old widow became obsessed with a question she could neither answer nor avoid. "Why?" she tearfully asked, "Why did this happen to me?" She asked it over and over, night after night, as she lay sleepless and alone in her bed. It was the only prayer she was able to pray. She tried to pray the types of prayers she thought people were supposed to pray in similar situations, prayers for comfort and strength to face her difficulties. But she could never finish those prayers. In mid-sentence she would fill with anguish, and the only words that came were the lone words that expressed how she truly felt. "Why, God? Why me?" she cried. No answer came, and after such moments she was consumed with a dark cloud of gloom which made even worse her sense that life was no longer worth living.

Cynthia and Mike had built their marriage and family life on faith. There was never any question about how the family would spend Sundays. They all went to Sunday School and Church, and when they were old enough the children also went to the youth group on Sunday evenings. Cynthia and Mike had participated in Bible study groups for many years, and had a serious, though sporadic, devotional life. The family prayed together at mealtime, and both parents had been conscientious about helping the children deal with life challenges in the context of faith.

Cynthia knew, as everyone does, that life can bring sudden and unexpected tragedy. But she never really believed it could happen to her. She always had a rather simple faith, uncomplicated by serious doubts or questions. Cynthia would not have admitted it, but deep inside her being she believed that because she, Mike, and the children were a family of faith, God had placed some kind of protective shield around them. As far back as she could remember, she had thought if she did her part, God would protect her and those close to her from harm. Intellectually she knew better. But in her heart of hearts, she was convinced that as long as she was not a bad person, bad things would not happen to her. At least she had believed that until Mike died. Now she did not know what to believe.

For a long time, Cynthia did not tell anyone about her spiritual struggle. It occurred to her that she might speak with a friend from church, or her pastor, about her questioning. She played out the scenario in her mind, but soon rejected the idea as too risky. She decided neither of them likely would understand what she was going through. She would get no satisfying answers, she predicted, only painful feelings of being judged for what she already had come to believe was her inadequate faith. Cynthia chose to suffer alone, and continued to ask "Why?", night after night.

One weekend when Cynthia's three-year-old grandson was visiting her, she found herself irritated because the child was asking her *why* about almost everything. And when she answered as best she could, he would again ask "Why?".

Toward the end of the weekend, when Cynthia had tried to answer, as best she could, a long list of her grandson's "why" questions, she turned the table on him. "Why do you ask "Why?" so much?" she asked him.

He became silent for a long time, frowned, stuck out his bottom lip in a pout, and in a rather pitiful voice said, "I don't know."

"Well, I will tell you a secret." Cynthia said softly, "Sometimes when you ask 'Why?' I don't know either." Needless to say, only a few minutes passed before she was bombarded by another series of *why* questions.

Cynthia doubted that a three-year-old was capable of the kind of reflection which she was demanding with her challenge to him. But she thought a person of her own mature years certainly ought to be. "So," Cynthia asked herself, "Why is it that I keep asking 'Why?' "

Cynthia had been struggling alone with her questioning for several weeks, when Ruth, an old college friend Cynthia had not thought about in years, called to express condolences. Ruth told Cynthia she had heard from a mutual acquaintance about Mike's death. She had lost her own husband to kidney disease almost two years earlier. She suggested the two of them get together to renew their friendship. Cynthia eagerly accepted the offer. A few days later, the two of them met at a local sandwich shop for lunch.

After the two widows shared their accounts of loss and talked about the differences in impact between a sudden death and a slow dying, Cynthia shared with Ruth her obsession with the question *Why?*.

"So you are a *why baby* too," Ruth said. "I certainly know where you are coming from. You have lots of company. Been there, done that."

"So what's the answer?" Cynthia asked. "I need someone just please to tell me why this happened to me. Why did Mike have to die?"

"Let me ask you something," Ruth responded gently. "What are you really asking when you ask, 'Why?' and *why* do you ask such a question? What kind of answer are you expecting? Can you conceive of an answer that would satisfy you or take away your pain, if you were convinced it was true?"

Cynthia had reflected on this same question at some length following her grandson's visit. She still did not know how to answer it.

"Look," Ruth said, "Nothing is more natural than to ask 'Why?' when a tragedy befalls us. People try to comfort us by telling us 'It is God's will,' or 'things happen for a reason,' all of which may be true in some unfathomable way. But such answers only cause us to ask more questions. When people said that to me, I wanted to say, 'Why is it God's will? And what possible reason could there be?' You see, the thing other people don't understand, unless they have been through something similar, is that we don't really want an explanation."

"Then what are we looking for?" Cynthia asked.

"We would love to turn back the clock and restore things to the way they used to be. That is what we really want. But we know that can never happen, because life doesn't work that way. So when we ask the *why* question, we don't expect an answer. One of the things we are doing is expressing a desire for our emotional pain and our feelings of abandonment to be validated."

"We are also registering a protest. We protest against a universe in which such awful things happen. We protest against the injustice of a world where such things happen to the good and decent people we love. We protest against a God who, if He does not directly cause these things to happen, He allows them to happen. We feel some great cosmic mistake has been made, and we can't fix it. All we can do is express the pain it has caused."

"I think I understand what you are getting at, but I don't think I ever expected to live in a world where nothing bad ever happens," Cynthia said. "I just want to know 'Why me?'"

"Of course you do. But it's the same deal. We feel we are somehow entitled to a free ride. By virtue of showing up in life, or living morally, or being religious, we think nothing bad is ever supposed to happen to us. We have the illusion that this is the natural order of things. When we are children, we are told if we are bad we will be punished, but if we are good we will be rewarded. We don't think about the real world out there, beyond the security of our homes, that doesn't play by those rules."

Ruth paused for a moment and then continued. "After my Tom passed away, I went into a serious state of self-pity. One day, after many months of asking 'Why me?', it hit me. 'Why *not* me?' We live in a world where a lot of bad stuff goes down every day. Did I have any more right to a life free of tragedy than anyone else? What kind of narcissistic pride is that? Jesus said the rain falls on both the just and the unjust, and I take that to mean it does so whether it is a gentle rain needed for crops to grow or a terrible destructive flood. It isn't personal, even though it affects me very personally."

"I also had another insight along the way. When everything was *going great*, I didn't think to ask 'Why me?' I only did that after it all was taken from me. The whole time Tom and I were together, I took our wonderful life for granted. I don't think I appreciated all those precious moments we had together. But after they were gone, I sure grieved their loss. It has taken a lot of time. But I now thank God for the wonderful times we shared. I realize today that I grieved so greatly because I loved and was loved so much. How blessed I am to have had such a wonderful marriage. Now, I try each day to appreciate the important relationships in life I still have."

"I don't know why Tom was taken from me," Ruth continued, "and I don't know why Mike was taken from you. And I'm fairly certain that neither does anybody else, except God, and sometimes, in my weaker moments, I am not so sure about God. All I know is that we don't ask *Why* unless we are confronted by a mystery. When we are confronted by a life-changing loss, we are dealing with the mysterious nature of life and of God. We want to take the mystery out of the mystery, but there is no way to do that."

"So does that mean you have stopped asking *Why*", Cynthia asked.

"To be perfectly honest," Ruth responded, "not entirely. But I have done a lot of praying for the ability to accept the things in life over which I have no control. And while my cry of 'Why?' has gone unanswered, God has helped me make progress in coming to terms with my situation. I ask different questions now. I ask questions like, 'What now?' 'What am I supposed to do with my life?' 'What do those around me who are still with me need from me?' For me, these questions feel a lot more productive than the *why* question. So I continue to pray for guidance and direction, and I feel that is starting to happen. In fact, I think that is why I called you. I had the strongest feeling when I heard about your loss, that I should get together with you."

A few days later, Cynthia awoke from a nap on the couch, with an overwhelming sense that she no longer was questioning God. God was now questioning her. She was not sure whether she had dreamed it, or whether it had just come to her in the twilight between a deep slumber and a waking state. But she heard the question quite clearly, nonetheless. "What now Cynthia?" "What now?"

A little more than a year later, Cynthia was asked to teach her adult Sunday School lesson. When she discovered the lesson was to be about the Old Testament character, Job, whose family and wealth were taken from him in sudden tragedy, she smiled and thought to herself, "God has quite a sense of humor."

Cynthia told the class that Sunday morning the story of her journey and her questioning. And she told them about the fateful conversation with her friend Ruth.

Speaking to the class from her notes, Cynthia said, "The question *Why?* is not only a *natural* one, but it probably is an *essential* one for our spiritual growth in times of profound tragedy. It is our human cry when we are wounded in spirit by an overwhelming loss. Tragic events overwhelm us. They disorient us. Before they happen, life makes sense to us. Afterwards, all our assumptions about the meaning of existence are called into question. When we find ourselves asking 'Why?', we are expressing our desire for life once more to make sense to us. We are longing for our faith in the goodness of God and our confidence in God's care to be restored. Asking 'Why?' can be an expression of abandonment, and, at the same time, it can be the beginning of a more realistic and profound faith."

"The Biblical character Job dramatizes a person desperately attempting to hold on to an inadequate faith which failed to account for the reality of real life experience. Whatever his sin, Job knew his suffering was exceedingly out of proportion to the events that had befallen him.

> *'If I have sinned, what have I done to you,*
> *O watcher of men?*
> *Why have you made me your target?*
> *Have I become a burden to you?'*
> *(Job 7:20 NIV)*

Job was broken by the weight of his losses. His tragedy was too great to fit into his old theology. He was forced to question everything, all his assumptions about life and faith. He begged God to put him out of his misery and just let him die. And when that didn't happen, he dared to question God's wisdom and justice. In the great climax of that drama, God turned the tables. God questioned Job for assuming the creature could understand, question and judge the Creator of all that is. And Job learned, as countless others have learned, that after tragedy strikes, nothing is ever the same again. But there can be a new beginning."

"For persons of faith who ask, as I did, the question 'Why me?', it is important to recognize that our questioning is a longing for healing. When we understand that our deepest desire is for God to acknowledge our devastation, we are able to transform our questioning into a prayer for healing. And when we begin to seek healing, we are on our way to a recovery, which will benefit not only us, but also those around us who need us to be there for *them* in times of difficulty. That is what happened to my friend Ruth. And because she had made that journey, it has happened to me as well. Ruth and I never found answers to our questions of why our life-mates were taken from us so early. But we have experienced something else that we have come to believe to be far more beneficial."

"O Lord my God, I called to you for help and you healed me." (Psalm 30:2)

Chapter 6:
Who Pushed Humpty Dumpty?

"But ask the animals, and they will teach you,
or the birds of the air, and they will tell you;
or speak to the earth, and it will teach you,
or let the fish of the sea inform you.
Which of these does not know
that the hand of the Lord has done this?"
(Job 12:7-9 NIV)

Anger

As we have seen, the questions *why?* and *why me?* often arise from the feeling that a terrible personal loss was not fair. When this perception persists, and we remain unwilling to accept the reality of our personal tragedies, we may attempt to place blame, and enter a time of anger.

For the most part, people are unlikely to become angry when their losses conform to their expectations about the natural patterns of life. When we lose a parent who has reached a normal life expectancy, sorrow may be profound, but it probably will not be accompanied by anger. And when a loved one has gone through much suffering, and death finally comes, we are much more inclined to have feelings of relief than of anger.

On the other hand, anger is a very common reaction when people die long before their expected times. When a young child's life has been taken by a disease, or a teenager has drowned, feelings of anger are to be expected. They also are likely to occur when careless, selfish, and irresponsible actions have brought about our losses. Grief over the infidelity of a mate often manifests itself as anger. And almost always we will react with anger, if our personal tragedies have resulted from malicious acts, such as a terrorist attack, a rape, or a murder.

Such diverse circumstances can explain why an individual who has experienced several seasons of grief over the years, may have become angry during some of them, but not during others. If we have negotiated successfully periods of anger during earlier seasons of grief, we also may find we are less likely to become angry when facing losses later in life. Yet even then, some types of tragedies are likely to trigger an angry response.

We have observed in earlier chapters that denial, escape, victimism, and questioning can have positive benefits. We also have recognized that they carry with them temptations and great risks. The same can be said for anger.

THE GIFT OF ANGER

Anger is a powerful emotion intended by God for the well-being of the human family. As the sound of a rattler warns an intruder not to step on a venomous snake, so expressions of anger can have positive results. They may tell those who might do us harm that we will not easily be victimized. They may remind would-be bullies and predators to consider the possible consequences their actions might bring upon themselves.

Among many of God's creatures, when a threat is encountered, anger transforms fear into courage. Anger gives strength to the weak, and at times makes possible the defeat of a more powerful enemy. Ordinary people in frightening situations can become heroes because of their anger. A regular foot soldier who has been filled with fury by the death of a buddy at the hands of an enemy, has been known to lead an attack, and to turn the tide of battle. Or one thinks of a petite woman who, having become possessed by rage, successfully fights off her much larger attacker.

Anger is a motivator. It is a potent weapon for challenging injustice and righting wrongs. The Old Testament prophets angrily denounced the unfaithfulness and wrongdoing of the people of Israel. When Jesus saw the moneychangers in the Temple, he drove them out in what appears to have been a state of righteous anger.

When we are grieving a loss, anger can motivate us to transcend self-pity, to abandon the victim role, and to take much needed actions. As we will see in Chapter 9, angry feelings are sometimes the impetus for activism which addresses serious problems and a stimulus for efforts to help others avoid similar suffering.

A DANGEROUS EMOTION

While sometimes it may be a good thing, *there is not a more dangerous emotion than anger.* It is a wild force within us which has to be tamed and guided before it can be helpful. Otherwise it may have terrible consequences for ourselves, for others, and for faith. The danger becomes real when our anger controls us, rather than being controlled by us. And the longer we remain stuck in an angry state of mind, the more dangerous it becomes.

Psychologists tell us that anger is a basic human emotion. It can be triggered spontaneously when we are confronted by a challenging situation. This often happens when something or someone prevents us from realizing a desire. This automatic response sends chemicals throughout our bodies prompting us briefly to *lose our tempers.* But if this response lasts more than a minute or two, it is because we have decided to continue to be angry. When we feel these rushes of anger, we have choice. We can choose to allow them to continue and thereby release more anger chemicals into our systems. Or we can decide to allow these spontaneous responses to melt away. If we do so, the flush of anger will subside within a few moments.

But if we allow it to continue unabated, anger can be like an evil spirit which possesses us, and stresses us, and destroys us from within. It can be destructive to our health. It can blind us, so that we cannot see the beauty and goodness of the world. It can turn us into bitter and joyless people.

Anger often destroys relationships, because anger and love cannot long coexist within us. Anger can stand in the way of the forgiveness and the reconciliation necessary for healing. It can block us from the peace God wants to restore in our hearts. As long as we continue angrily blaming ourselves, blaming others, and blaming God for the occasions of our grief, we will not be able to succeed on our journeys toward recovery.

"WHY ARE YOU ANGRY?"

In the Biblical narrative of Cain and Abel, we are told each of the brothers offered sacrifices to God. Abel's sacrifice was said to be pleasing to God, but Cain's was not. Cain became very angry and downcast. Cain had an expectation that his sacrifice would result in some kind of personal benefit. He observed Abel, his brother, receiving this reward, while he did not. Cain reacted with anger and pouting to what he thought was unfair treatment. Cain was furious that life could be so unfair.

Neither blessings nor sufferings appear to be handed out in this world in a fair fashion. Some lives are much more filled with tragedy and pain than are others. We have difficulty understanding why those who do evil may prosper, and those who do good things may suffer. And we not only ask *why* life is this way, but sometimes we respond, as Cain responded, by becoming angry.

The unfairness of life may be felt especially when tragedy strikes in a life of faith. Whatever the reasons for our difficulties, we may feel, as did Cain, that the sacrifices we have made through our faithful living have been in vain. And after suffering a major loss, we too may respond with anger and pouting, just as we did when we were children and felt we had been treated unfairly. Sometimes, just as Cain became angry with his brother, we may direct our anger toward other children of God. For example, a couple, having lost a child to disease, may become angry and resentful toward one another, though neither is to blame.

In the story, God asks Cain, "Why are you angry? Why are you downcast?". If we pay attention, whenever we find ourselves angry and pouting, God is asking us those same questions. "Why are you angry?" "Why are you so upset?" Is it because we feel life has been unfair to us? Do we blame God because we feel we are being unjustly punished? Do we feel someone else needs to be punished, so we might feel better? Or do we blame ourselves, and feel we deserve to be punished?

No matter how we answer these questions, we are reminded by this story that the emotion of anger is accompanied by great danger. *When we sense that God is asking us, "Why are you angry?", it is important to understand that such a moment is an opportunity to grow spiritually and to take the next step on our journey of grief and faith.* Instead of reflecting on God's question and allowing it to change his attitude, Cain aimed his anger at Abel and killed him.

OVERCOMING ANGER

It is clear, then, that anger can be a powerful emotion threatening to consume us, as wild flames can threaten to consume a house. But how does a person fight the flames of anger?

The first step is to become willing to let our anger go. That sounds easier than it is, because we may have become seriously attached to our anger. Angry feelings are addictive. We cling to them the same way we persist in bad habits which threaten our health. We tend to gain a perverse enjoyment from them.

When that is the case, it is important for people of faith to realize we need God's help in order to extinguish the flames of anger. Our first prayer must be for the willingness to let it go, to be free of all resentment toward *ourselves*, toward *others*, and toward *God*. And then, when God has made us willing, we need to ask God to remove that anger, so we can continue on our journey toward a life beyond grief.

Carlos

The high school memorial service was a well-attended tribute to a popular young man. Juan, a sixteen-year-old honor student, died when the speeding car in which he was riding ran off the road and flipped into a tree. The boy's parents, Carlos and Maria, though broken-hearted, were justly proud. Nearly everyone in the community had paid their respects in one way or another, and it was obvious their neighbors and friends grieved their loss with them.

Soon after the boy was buried, with the assistance of their priest, Father Fuentes, Carlos and Maria dedicated their child's old bedroom to serve as a shrine of remembrance. There they created an altar decorated with pictures of Juan, and with candles, flowers and a crucifix.

It was not long, however, before Carlos began avoiding the shrine. His grief had begun with efforts to honor his son's life, but it rapidly had turned into anger. Carlos was consumed with an indignant sense of the injustice of what had happened. He felt a compelling desire to blame whoever was responsible.

At first, Carlos decided he himself was to blame. He became obsessed with his own transgressions over the years. He had gone to confession and attended Mass far less frequently than Maria. He thought about how, in his younger years, he had been prone to many of the vices that God despises. As a middle-aged man, he had continued to have what the priest called "impure thoughts." Sometimes he had too much to drink. "Surely," he thought, "God is punishing me for my sins."

For several months, Carlos loathed himself and tortured himself with a series of *What ifs*. "What if I had been a better man, a better father, a better husband?" "What if I had spent more time with Juan, or had been stricter with him, like my father was with me." "Would any of these things have made a difference?" "Would my son still be alive, if I had done something different?" He wasn't sure what he possibly could have done differently. But Carlos became so angry with himself that he put his fist through the plasterboard wall of his kitchen.

It was a dramatic gesture, but it did not put an end to the questions. "What if I had said 'no' when Juan asked if he could ride in his friend's car to the game?" "What if I had driven him myself, instead of staying home to watch television?" Carlos secretly had been glad he did not have to drive Juan to the game that night. Now he hated himself for it.

Maria tried to assure Carlos that the death was not his fault. But instead of being reassured, Carlos became angrier. He turned on Maria, and began to make her the focus of his wrath. It was not that Carlos believed Maria had contributed directly to their son's death. It was just that she was there. He began to yell at her about the smallest matters. Maria was not the kind of woman to let such behavior pass. She was skilled at giving back what was given to her. The arguments became intensely hurtful. They quarreled about anything and everything. Within a few months, Maria, for the first time in their years of marriage, was considering leaving Carlos.

The tension between them soon began to ease, however, as Carlos found another focus for his anger. He had never liked Marcus, the friend who was driving the car the night his son was killed. He always thought Marcus was spoiled and headed for trouble. And Carlos was well aware Marcus had been drinking and driving too fast at the time of the accident.

Despite all of this, Carlos, along with Maria, initially felt a great deal of sympathy for their son's friend. Marcus, after all, had been injured seriously himself, and might not ever walk again. But after many miserable months, when Carlos' anger at himself and Maria had brought him no consolation, all remaining sympathy for the boy abruptly ended. In the weeks that followed, the more Carlos thought about it, the more he blamed Marcus. Marcus became the primary object of Carlos' wrath.

One Sunday, after Mass, Carlos saw Marcus being pushed in a wheelchair by his parents. They were on the way to their van in the church parking lot. Carlos lost it. He went up to the boy and stood over him. With face red, body shaking, and in a voice loud enough for all those leaving the church that day to hear, he shouted curses and accusations. The shocked teen began to cry. Marcus' father stepped between the two and challenged Carlos. A fight was barely avoided, when several parishioners quickly intervened.

For weeks, Carlos' thoughts were obsessed with wishing harm to Marcus. When Marcus' DWI charges finally came to court, Carlos was there. He wanted the court to put Marcus in prison for Juan's death. The judge allowed Carlos to speak, but his words had no effect on the outcome. Marcus' lawyer already had worked out a plea bargain with the county prosecutor. The eighteen-year-old was convicted of DWI and reckless driving. His license was suspended for a year and he had to pay a fine.

Carlos now became furious at the justice system. He began to refer to it as the *injustice* system. Every representative of government authority suddenly became Carlos' enemy. Once, when he was stopped by a police officer for a traffic violation, Carlos verbally exploded. It almost ended in an arrest.

Carlos no longer raged at Maria. But things were not the same between them. That remained true even after their financial windfall. A personal injury lawyer had approached Carlos and Maria shortly after the accident, and eventually the automobile insurance company covering Marcus' car settled with the parents for just over a million dollars. Even after the attorney received his agreed upon percent, there remained enough to pay off all the debts, to buy a new car, and to buy a house in a more affluent neighborhood. But despite his improved surroundings, Carlos remained angry.

Months turned into years. Carlos' anger, which had been focused on himself and others, now was aimed consciously at God. Carlos stopped going to church altogether. He began to question everything he ever had been taught about God. "How can God be good, if God lets such bad things happen?", he asked. "If God is able to perform miracles, why didn't God perform one that night?" Carlos now believed God was the one who ultimately and truly was to blame for what had happened. And he was determined to live his own life as a protest against God's cruelty.

One day, at the secret request of Maria, the priest came by to visit. Carlos liked Father Fuentes, but he was not pleased to see him. "You are wasting your time, Father," Carlos said. "I refuse to believe in a God who allows such terrible things to happen. Juan had his whole life ahead of him. He did not deserve to die. He had not done anything wrong."

Carlos felt himself losing emotional control. He took a moment to regain his composure before continuing. "Father, I know I have done things wrong, but nothing so bad as to deserve this. And what kind of God would punish my son for my sins, anyhow? What kind of God would do this to our family? Don't waste your time on me, Father. I am so mad at God that I am sure God does not want anything to do with me. Go away, Father. There is nothing you can say that will make any difference."

"So you are angry with God," Father Fuentes said softly. "Do you think you are the first person ever to be angry with God? Do you think you are the only one who ever questioned God? As a priest, I can tell you that almost everyone in our parish who has ever experienced a tragedy has asked these questions, expressed these doubts, and felt such anger."

"Let me assure you, Carlos, God is used to this," the priest continued. "God can handle it just fine. But I am concerned about you. I am worried about what all this anger is doing to Carlos. I don't deny that anger occasionally can serve a good purpose. Anger at an injustice can motivate people to help end the suffering of others. And it is natural for us to go through some anger, when tragic things happen to us. It is part of the way we handle our grief. But you appear to have gotten yourself stuck in your anger. That is not a good thing for you Carlos, or for Maria, or for anyone else close to you."

"That may be the case, Father," Carlos replied with sharpness in his voice. "But I don't think I can help it, and I don't really care. I told you, Father, you are wasting your time on me."

When the priest left that day, Carlos assumed he would not see him again, at least for a very long time. But he had underestimated Father Fuentes' persistence. A week later the priest was back.

"Last time we spoke," Father Fuentes began, "you said you didn't care about what your anger is doing to you. Maybe you don't care. I don't know. But what I truly would like to know is whether you care about *anything* right now. What *do* you care about, Carlos? You are not the only hurt soul in this world. There are others hurting all around you. Have you considered how much pain Maria is in, because she also lost a son? Have you thought for one moment how you have multiplied that pain, because you are so angry? And have you considered that our parish is filled with people who also are suffering? Maybe not about the death of a son, but with suffering that is real too?"

A flush of fresh anger came over Carlos. "I know there is suffering in the world! That is what makes me so angry with God!", the grieving father shouted as he waved his hands in the air. "Why did God make a world in which all this suffering happens? And don't say it's because of sin. Because I know there are a lot of terrible sinners out there doing just fine, and a lot of good people in this world who have had very bad things happen to them."

"You are right about that, Carlos," the priest responded. "Our Lord once was asked whether some men, who were killed when a tower fell on them, were worse sinners than others. The Lord told his questioners that those men had not sinned any more than anyone else. Sometimes bad stuff happens way out of proportion to people's sins. Even the Lord himself knew terrible suffering on the cross."

"That is the way life is, Carlos," the priest continued. "Bad things happen. Make no mistake. Sometimes it *is* because of our sin. And sometimes it is because of the sin of others. But sometimes tragedies just *happen*. As we learned as children in the nursery rhyme about Humpty Dumpty, sometimes there is a great fall, and things are so broken that they can never be put back together again. But it is not always because somebody pushed. Sometimes there is nobody to blame. Does God allow these bad things to happen? You bet God does. Do I understand why? Not really. A lot of people try to explain these things, but the truth is that we human beings are incapable of understanding the ways of God."

"But Carlos, we *are* capable of understanding that when bad things happen to us, God wants us to do something with our lives besides sit around and feel sorry for ourselves, or wallow in our anger. I am going to ask you what I believe God is asking you. 'Have you learned anything from your loss? Have you allowed yourself to grow spiritually through your suffering?' You say you can't help being angry. I know you have blamed God. But have you called upon God to help you heal? Have you asked God to take away your anger? Have you opened your heart and let God comfort you? Have you availed yourself of his Sacraments?"

"You say you are upset about all the tragedy in the world. So, if you are so concerned about all this suffering in the world, Carlos, what are you doing about it? Do you really care, or are you too busy enjoying your resentment? Are you going to continue to indulge your resentment until it destroys your soul? Resentment possesses and consumes those who allow it to flourish. It is a selfish, perverted pleasure that does away with all hope and happiness. But you already know this in your heart."

During the days that followed, Carlos attempted to dismiss the priest's words and not think about them. But he could not get them out of his mind. One Friday night, unable to focus on anything else, he tossed and turned sleeplessly, well into the early morning hours. Sometime before dawn, he slipped out of bed, and, for the first time in a very long time, he went to Juan's room. He knelt at the altar, lit some candles, and prayed.

He asked Juan to forgive him. He asked God to forgive him. He vowed he would ask Maria in the morning to forgive him. He prayed for the willingness to forgive Juan's friend, Marcus. He prayed for guidance, for spiritual growth, and that God would help him move beyond his anger so that he might be able again to feel the pain of others and help them. He prayed, through tears, for a long time. He finally went to bed, as dawn was breaking. He fell asleep without effort, and slept most of the day. It was his best sleep in a very long time.

The day after that, Carlos surprised Maria by attending Mass with her. He was still feeling estranged from God. But then something happened to him that helped him feel less so.

The reality that had angered Carlos more than anything during the years since Juan's death was that his son had died so young. Carlos was haunted by the consciousness of all Juan might have experienced and accomplished in the years that were snatched from him. Each time the grieving father thought about it, he was filled with resentment. "Fathers are not supposed to outlive their sons!", he had yelled during numerous outbursts around the house.

As Carlos participated in the Mass that day, his eyes were drawn to the large crucifix hanging behind and above the altar. His attention first focused on the nails in the hands and feet, and on the bleeding side. Then he looked at the face of Jesus. As he studied it, he realized, perhaps consciously for the first time, that Jesus had died a very young man. It occurred to Carlos, as he stared at that youthful face, that God knew better than anyone how he, Carlos, felt. In the midst of that insight, Carlos was aware of a warming in the region of his heart. A voice within him seemed to be saying, "God knows and God cares." It was a moment of healing. Carlos tried to conceal his tears from those around him.

A few Sundays later, he listened attentively to the priest's sermon. It was part of a series the priest was delivering on "The Seven Deadly Sins." And the topic of the day was "Anger." As Carlos listened, he suspected that Father Fuentes had prepared this sermon with a particular parishioner in mind.

"Whenever we find ourselves angry," Father Fuentes said, "our anger may have a deeper meaning than we might first assume. Is our anger aimed at ourselves, because we think we are the cause of some unfortunate event? Are we trying to resolve our grief by blaming someone else and seeking revenge? Or is our anger aimed at that Mysterious Power which created all of life and made it the way it is? Is our anger a manifestation of defiance toward life, and, as such, a deep seated resentment toward God?"

"Most of us," Father Fuentes said, "experience anger as we grieve personal tragedy. We feel if someone could be punished for what happened, healing would follow. When we direct anger toward ourselves, we feel the need for punishment. We often engage in behavior we know will bring us pain. We do so, not in spite of the consequences, but in order to achieve them. The belief that we deserve to be punished becomes a self-fulfilling prophecy."

"When anger is focused on others, the desire for revenge reigns. Families who have lost a loved one to murder, often believe closure and healing will come only when the responsible party has been convicted and executed. Justice, in such circumstances, has important social benefits. Yet we are all familiar with television interviews of victim's families after an execution in which it is evident that the longed-for closure and healing did not happen. The problem is, people look for external events and solutions to heal them. They fail to recognize that the problem is not an external one. Others legitimately may be to blame for our personal tragedies, but we are responsible for how we deal with them, nonetheless."

Carlos flinched as he remembered his confrontation with Marcus. It had not been one of his prouder moments.

"When our anger is aimed at God," Father Fuentes continued, "we believe we will find resolution for our pain in the rightness of our position. We believe our anger is justified because we have experienced what we believe to be the injustice of God. Now it is difficult to war with God. As Job recognized, there is no way to win in a direct challenge to the Almighty. So when we are angry with God, we usually take an indirect approach. We may protest, as Job did, by asking God to end our lives, to finish the job, so to speak. And sometimes we displace that anger on some other person or group of persons."

"When we are consumed with anger, whether at ourselves, others, or God," Father Fuentes continued, "we are dealing with a powerful force that must be removed, before it takes over our lives, destroys us, and wreaks havoc in the lives of those around us. If not spiritually treated, anger can destroy the soul. But before resentments can be banished and healing occur, forgiveness and repentance are required."

Carlos listened closely to this part. It had taken many years, but now he was ready to hear what was being said.

"It is not easy for a person of faith to admit being possessed by toxic resentments," Father Fuentes told his parishioners. "We believe ourselves to be good people who have excellent reasons to be angry. We have to justify our resentments in order to maintain them. Consequently, in order to experience healing, it is necessary for us to let go of our justifications for our resentments. That, of course, is easier said than done. But that is where genuine repentance comes in."

"Persons of faith know in their hearts that all resentments are, in reality, resentment towards God. For even when we are angry with ourselves and other human beings, we are angry with God's children, those whom God has created and loves. And as persons of faith, we also know we are called to repentance for our spiritual failures, in order that we may find peace with God and become compassionate, as God is compassionate. Repentance means *to turn away* and *to let go.* In repentance we acknowledge our spiritual problems and ask God to assist us in removing them."

"We don't repent," the priest continued, looking directly at Carlos, "to accept responsibility for something we did not do. We repent because we take responsibility for attempting to justify our anger. We repent because we acknowledge we foolishly have tried to heal ourselves by blaming ourselves, and by blaming others. We repent because we have withheld forgiveness from others, despite the reality that we have received God's forgiveness. We repent because we recognize we have attempted to escape our creaturely status and to pass judgment on God, the Creator of all that is. We repent because we desire to be released from the anger we have allowed to take possession of us and which is destroying our souls."

"As persons of faith, we turn to God in prayer. We pray for forgiveness, and for the grace to forgive ourselves and others. We pray for those persons toward whom our anger has been directed. We pray to be restored to a loving relationship with God and with all our neighbors. We pray that our anger will be transformed into empathetic passion, so we may become instruments of God's love in alleviating the suffering around us. We pray that our grief will be healed by the One who desires to heal us and who is able to change our suffering into loving care toward others."

Carlos would not afterward remember the exact words of this sermon. But he would take them to heart. He began to pray the way Father Fuentes had suggested. In time, Carlos underwent a miraculous change of heart. And with this transformation came a change in his attitude toward Maria, toward Marcus and toward God. He felt a new peace, and he was able to know freedom from the terrible bitterness that had eaten away at his soul for so long.

Chapter 7:
Never Put A Period Where
a Comma Belongs

"We are hard pressed on every side, but not crushed; perplexed, but not in despair; persecuted but not abandoned; struck down, but not destroyed." *(2 Cor 4:8-9 NIV)*

Depression

When we think about a person in grief, we generally picture someone who is sorrowful and has a downcast demeanor. We may recall a particular friend or acquaintance whose eyes sometimes filled with tears at unexpected moments, and who occasionally wept convulsively.

As we have seen, there are many faces of grief which do not fit this stereotype. A person in denial, running away, feeling like a victim, questioning, or expressing anger, may not appear to be grieving. But those expressions of emotional pain are as valid, in their own periods of grief, as the emotions of sadness and depression are in theirs.

The stereotype of grief as depression fails to portray the diversity of the grieving process. Nevertheless, deep sadness is the most common of all the periods of grieving. It is also the most painful.

Tears

In our culture, crying tends to be associated with infants, and with weakness. We have been conditioned to believe it is wrong for adults to cry. Both men and women are likely to feel this way at times, but it is especially true for males. Simply put, tears are thought not to be manly.

So when we have tearful moments, or episodes of sobbing uncontrollably after a loss, we can feel foolish, embarrassed, and incapable of controlling our emotions. And when this happens, we become more depressed, because we feel that we are losing courage and control. Afterward, we may try even harder to hold back the tears, and in doing so, we may deny ourselves the kind of emotional release that can help us heal.

It is important to understand it is natural and healthy to experience tearful episodes in the midst of our sorrows. In the case of the death of a loved one, such moments may be occasioned by memory-evoking events such as anniversaries, birthdays or holidays, by places where special moments once were shared, and by objects associated with the deceased, such as a pair of glasses or strands of hair in a comb. It is normal to have such tearful moments, even many years after a loss. At such times we re-experience the pain and the loneliness of our earlier time of grieving.

Grieving tears, we are told by scientists, are chemically different from other tears. When we are in emotional pain, our bodies produce chemicals and hormones that dramatically lower our mood. Crying releases pain relievers and mood elevators into the bloodstream. Tears chemically sooth our sadness. That is the physiological reason we feel better after crying.

There is also a psychological and spiritual effect. Crying is a bodily means of releasing the internal pressure of emotional pain. We cry to release our suffering and to cleanse our inner visions. Through tears, we symbolically wash away our pain. Such *baths* may be needed frequently for a period of time and occasionally for the rest of our lives.

It is interesting to contrast our current western cultural attitude toward the shedding of tears with that of Biblical peoples. In ancient Israel, men and women wept openly during times of intense feelings. The stories of Jacob and Esau, and of Joseph and his brothers, tell of weeping during emotionally charged moments of reconciliation. And tears are associated with grief throughout the Scriptures. We read of David crying over the death of his son Absalom, of Jeremiah's fountain of tears over the fall of Jerusalem, of Jesus weeping over the sins of that same city, of the bitter tears of Simon Peter after he had denied Jesus three times, and of Mary weeping at Jesus' tomb, to mention only a few relevant passages.

That tears are associated with all kinds of human suffering in the Bible is underscored by the promises of hope we find there. "Weeping may remain for a night, but rejoicing comes in the morning" (Psalm 30:5b NIV). "Those who sow with tears will reap with songs of joy" (Psalm 126:5 NIV). "And God shall wipe away all tears from their eyes; and there shall be no more death, neither sorrow, nor crying, neither shall there be any more pain: for the former things are passed away" (Rev. 21:4 *NIV*).

DEPRESSION AND HEALING

Not only can tears have a salving effect, depression itself can have healing benefits. When we are physically sick, our bodies warn us that we need to rest and to take care of ourselves for a while, until we begin to recover. When we are very ill, we often find we are unable to continue with all but the most basic activities of daily living, and we may discover we even need the assistance of others in order to deal with those. Rest and additional sleep are important for successful physical healing.

But when in time we show signs of feeling better, an indication that we are beginning the process of recovery, it is important for us to begin to resume normal activities. If we remain in the sick role, we will lose ground physically, and we may eventually lose the capacity to get better.

Feelings of depression are comparable to the way we experience ourselves when we are physically sick. In addition to *physical* energy, the challenges of daily living require *emotional* and *spiritual* energy. A depressed person may not feel like getting out of bed in the morning, bathing, grooming, getting dressed, or going out. This inclination toward personal neglect is likely to be accompanied by an absence of motivation to do the simplest of household duties.

A person in deep sorrow also may experience intense loneliness which feels like abandonment. And this may be true even when the personal tragedy is not about the loss of a loved one. Our feelings of aloneness arise in part from the sense that nobody knows what we are going through. We believe others are unable to understand. And if they really did know how we feel, we think they might not love us, or might not approve of our struggle.

As bad as all of this may seem, depression can be a necessary stage on our journey toward recovery. As the tiredness and weakness we feel when we are physically ill can play a positive role in bodily healing, emotional depression serves a similar function in our lives when we have been traumatized by a loss. *Melancholy can force us to slow down, to reduce our activities, to increase our rest, and to distinguish between the important things in our lives and the unimportant ones.*

DANGEROUS DEPRESSION

As is true for other stages of grief, it is important to remember that any potential benefit from a depressed mood is short-lived. Just as the prolonging of the sick role can lead to further loss of health, so the extension of a season of sadness beyond its appointed time has the potential for great harm.

While it is normal and sometimes necessary for us to be depressed during grief, a tragic loss can trigger in some persons a serious episode of an underlying depressive illness. Persons with feelings of worthlessness, hopelessness, excessive guilt, and thoughts of suicide, may be suffering biochemically from a psychiatric disorder. If such symptoms are present, it is important to consult a physician, because clinical depression generally requires treatment with counseling and medication in order to address the underlying conditions. In such cases medication should not be seen as an alternative to the grieving journey, but, when medically appropriate, as an important tool for surviving the darkest days of grief.

Our concern here, however, is not so much the need that some of us may have for medical attention, as it is the need all of us may have for spiritual guidance. Many of us who become stuck in depression, do not do so because of an underlying psychiatric condition, but because we are unwilling to continue our journey toward accepting the reality of our losses.

While depression can move us toward healing, it also may bring with it the spiritual temptation to give up on life. To take overt action on suicidal thoughts usually is an indication of clinical depression. But there also are other forms of giving up that may tempt any of us during the sadness of our grief. This *hidden suicide* may be expressed as the long-term decision not to feel, not to put forth effort, not to do anything but muddle through each day.

Once we decide life is not worth living, we may make the decision each moment of each day to give in to depression, to let others take care of us, and to yield to a life without the possibility of hope or joy. Or we may take an opposite approach. Instead of shutting down, we may adopt a high-risk lifestyle. This sometimes takes the form of pursuing daily oblivion through immoral behaviors and mind-altering substances, without regard to consequences. This hopelessness, this giving up, may be an indication of clinical depression, as well. But when there is no underlying mental disease, it is more likely to be a case of spiritual despair.

Depression is hazardous, because every day we are in its grip it becomes more difficult to rise above it. Depression can become a downward spiral. When our mood remains low for very long, we are in danger of falling into despair and becoming stuck in perpetual sadness. Just as it may be impossible to climb out of clinical depression without medical assistance, so it is most unlikely to escape the pit of spiritual despair on our own. We need help, and asking for it is a sign of strength. *We may not be able at times to get out of despair on our own, but we are able to seek help and to ask for it.* To do so is a faith response. Not to do so can be a deadly form of unfaith.

DEPRESSION AND THE SPIRITUAL JOURNEY

Depression may be dangerous, but it also can serve as a catalyst for spiritual growth. In order to grow spiritually, we need to feel our emotional pain, we need to be able to identify with the suffering of others. Depression can make that happen. And it can serve to detach us from everyday concerns and awaken us to our spiritual essence. The spiritual function of grief is to cleanse the soul of bitter feelings, not to multiply them. That is why it is important during times of depression not to neglect the practices of our faith.

When we fall into despair, the help we need might come to us through the Scriptures, through a sermon, during a time of prayer, or in some other moment when we have opened our inner selves to God's healing. Or it might come from a spiritual counselor, or a person of faith who is a good friend. That is one of the reasons we need to maintain our friendships, even when we do not feel like doing so.

In any case, we need to hold on to the promises of our faith. We need to hold on to hope, and not let go. We need to ask God for help and to trust that it will come in God's time. And we need to get out into the world and start engaging with life. For as long as we have the gift of life, there is life to be lived and a journey to be completed.

Angela

For the fourth time in a little more than three years, nineteen-year-old Angela was involuntarily committed to a psychiatric facility. Once again she had attempted suicide. It was a near miss.

The first time Angela had shown signs of suicidal behavior was a few weeks before her sixteenth birthday. It had been little more than a dangerous gesture in which she made small cuts on her wrists, too superficial to do any damage. All of her later attempts, however, had been in the form of serious pill overdoses, combinations of over-the-counter pain relievers and the medications that psychiatrists had prescribed for her depression. Fortunately, she had been found, on each of those occasions, before it was too late. She had been rushed to an emergency room, where her stomach was pumped, and she was admitted for observation. After a couple of days, she was transported each time in a police vehicle for psychiatric hospital admission.

Those hospitalizations had ranged from two to four weeks each. In the months between hospitalizations, Angela spent much of her time engaging in behaviors designed to kill her emotional pain. She drank a lot and often drove while intoxicated. She also smoked a considerable amount of pot, and spent long hours in a stoned stupor. She had engaged in casual sex with men she met in clubs and bars so many times that she had lost count. But none of it worked. Each time her pain persisted, and, eventually, there was another suicide attempt.

Angela's behavior was a far cry from her earlier teen years. She had been an active participant and leader in her church youth group. She had taken several mission trips to Appalachia and to hurricane damaged areas, to help people repair and build back their homes. She had attended spiritual retreats and Christian concerts with her group. She was respected for her sincere faith and for her exemplary behavior. At school she was regarded as someone who was a little too well behaved, but likable nevertheless.

Then Angela met Tony. She was fifteen-and-a-half at the time, and Tony had just turned eighteen. Tony was a freshman at a local university. He was strikingly handsome. He was fun loving, and he owned a car. Both Angela and Tony immediately were smitten. It was for each of them their first experience with the kind of love in which one constantly thinks about the other.

Because Angela was only fifteen, her parents were not happy about the relationship. Her father was particularly upset about it. But her mother insisted that Angela was mature for her age and that Tony was a nice young man. She was concerned that it might be a serious mistake to forbid their daughter from seeing him. Instead, they demanded considerable accountability for the time the two were together. They were not allowed to go out together often. When they were, Angela's parents insisted on knowing where the couple planned to go, who would be there, what they would be doing, and when, within strict curfew times, they would be home. And Tony and Angela did stick to the rules, for the most part. Then something happened that changed everything.

When Tony and Angela had been dating for about three months, her father came home unexpectedly to find the two of them having sex in Angela's bedroom. Her father exploded with anger, picked up the telephone and called the police. That call was like the hurling of a stone that, once thrown, could never be retrieved. Tony was arrested. Because of the age difference, and the laws concerning sex with a minor in their state, he was charged with sexual assault. During the arrest and incarceration, he was treated roughly by the police. He was fingerprinted. One of the arresting officers informed him that he could be sentenced to twenty years under state law, and, if convicted, he would be listed permanently on the sex offender registry.

Late that night, while alone in his cell, Tony tore his shirt and wrapped it into a makeshift rope. He hanged himself from the metal screen covering the overhead light fixture in his cell. By the time the guards found Tony, it was too late to revive him.

The night after Angela watched Tony's casket descend into the ground, Angela cut her wrists. When she emerged from the bathroom bleeding, her parents rushed her to the hospital.

More than three years later, on her fourth visit to the psychiatric hospital, something happened which again would change the course of Angela's life. The psychiatrist who was assigned to her was a young female resident. She took a special interest in Angela's case. After reviewing the record, she sat down to talk with Angela. In conversations over several days, she laid the groundwork for a therapeutic relationship.

One day, fully anticipating the answer that would be forthcoming, the psychiatrist asked Angela, "What is the worst thing that ever happened to you?" Angela's eyes filled with tears as she remembered Tony and recounted the circumstances of his death.

"How do you feel about Tony now?", the psychiatrist asked.

"I still love him and miss him."

"Is that all?"

"I feel like if it wasn't for me he would still be alive. And I am really mad at my Dad for calling the police on him."

"What else do you feel?"

After a long pause, she said, "I am really angry he did what he did. I know he was really upset about things, but he didn't have to kill himself."

" I will tell you what I am going to do", the young physician said. "I am going to give you some homework to do before tomorrow. I want you to write a letter to Tony. I want you to tell him how you feel about what he did. Can you do that?"

"I guess so," she replied.

Angela sat down that night in the visitor's lounge and began to write her letter. She started slowly. But soon the words burst forth from some long-locked chamber within her. She told Tony how much she loved and missed him. She told him how sorry she was for placing him in danger, and how responsible she felt because her father called the police on him. But then, with tears dripping on the page and smudging some of the words, she told Tony what he had done was stupid and selfish. She told him she knew he was in a lot of trouble. She knew he felt a lot of fear and emotional pain. But she also knew that, if he had not killed himself, he somehow could have gotten through it all. Other people had gotten through even worse things. She reminded him of soldiers coming home from war with arms and legs and eyes missing, who had chosen not to give up in the face of overwhelming odds.

"Why couldn't you see that your life was not over?" "Why couldn't you see it?" she wrote.

The next day she handed several limp pages to her therapist. The woman read the pages slowly before responding. "I see someone put a period where there should have been a comma," she said.

Angela looked embarrassed and puzzled. "I was never very good in English," she responded.

"Oh, I'm not talking about your punctuation. I'm talking about what you said to Tony. That is what you said, isn't it? Tony put a period in his life, where a comma belonged."

"I guess so." Angela responded uncertainly.

The therapist leaned forward, looked her patient in the eye, and spoke gently but firmly. "How about you Angela? Have you put a period in your life, where a comma belongs? I am not just talking about your attempts to kill yourself, though you have attempted to do exactly what Tony did, four different times. But you also have put a pretty effective period on your own life through your partying, your boozing, your drugging, and your sexual activity. You started all of this when you were fifteen. Because of the way you have chosen to handle your grief, you now are a nineteen-year- old stuck at the emotional maturity level of a fifteen-year-old. In fact, I take that back. You have regressed to the emotional state of a child who refused to recognize that life has legitimate limits, and in the process you have missed three good years of your life that you will never have back. Yes, what happened to *you* was a terrible thing. But you could have gotten through it if *you* had not decided your life was over."

This moment became a turning point in Angela's life. As she lay awake in her bed that night, she remembered how life had been for her before she started dating Tony. She remembered how she used to believe in God and that God had a purpose for her life. As she drifted off to sleep, she prayed for the first time in a very long time. She prayed that God would help her find her purpose.

The next day, Angela asked to see the hospital chaplain. The chaplain was a man in his forties, with kind eyes and a gentle voice. Angela had seen him on the wards during previous hospitalizations, but this was the first time she had spoken with him. She filled him in on her story and then said, " I have made such a mess of my life I don't know what to do now. I don't want to do what Tony did. I don't want to stop living, but I don't know how to start again. What do I need to do?"

The chaplain responded. "Unlike your boyfriend's self-destruction, or the way it would have been had you succeeded in taking your own life, you still have a life and you still have a future. You speak of your old love as if he were the only one who ever cared for you. I am betting you have people now who love you, who care for you, and who are hurting because you are hurting. We can't change the past. But we can change our relationship to the present. We can change the future and we can reach out to others for help."

"I just wish I could turn the clock back to that awful day and change what happened." Angela said.

"Have you ever heard of Marilyn Monroe?" the chaplain asked.

"I think so. Wasn't she that blonde actress who died of a drug overdose a long time ago?"

"That's right. Did you know that Marilyn Monroe had a terrible childhood? She was sexually abused as a child. She had a terrible mother. Later, after she had become a famous actress, she became engaged to a well-known playwright named Arthur Miller. She was very excited and happy at the time. As she was preparing for the wedding, some members of the press interviewed her. One of them, knowing about her troubled past, asked her, 'Miss Monroe, if you could, would you change anything about your life up to this point?' "

"The actress hesitated just a moment and then answered. 'Of course there are many things in my past I wish had not happened. I wouldn't want them to happen to anyone. But if by going back and changing one thing it would mean I would not be here today preparing for this wedding, I wouldn't change a thing.' At that moment Marilyn Monroe voiced a very important truth. Unfortunately, she later forgot about her own amazing insight."

"We all sometimes wish we could go back and change the past. I can think of several times I would have liked to have started over and made different decisions. Some of those times were major events in my life. But it doesn't work that way. And then, if I could go back and change something, my whole life would be different than it has been. I wouldn't be the chaplain at this hospital, and I wouldn't be sitting here with you right now. And Angela, I know in my heart today that I am exactly where I am supposed to be."

"Don't waste your energies trying to change the past," the chaplain continued. "There is a story in the Bible about the wife of a man named Lot who looked back at a disaster behind her and she turned into a pillar of salt. If we get hung up on the terrible things in our past, we can't change and move forward. We become like pillars of salt."

"A lot of young people do every day what you did, with very different results. It was not possible for you to have seen at the time what the outcome was going to be. But no matter how unwise or wrong our acts, no matter how tragic the result of our actions, the past is the past. You need to focus on living now, and on making the decisions now that are needed to turn your life around. And here is the miraculous truth about what God can do. God can take our crummy pasts, that we can't change, and use them for good, if we will let that happen."

"This, Angela," the chaplain continued, " is one of the most important themes of the Bible. The Bible mostly is about people who messed up. Some of them messed up again and again. But God kept giving them new chances to turn things around. Even when the results of their messing up were really bad, God found a way to give them another chance. It also tells us about people who had terrible things happen to them that were not their fault. Some things didn't happen because the people messed up. They just happened. Stuff happens in life. But God also was able to turn those things into good. Don't ask me how God does this. I can't understand it. But I have experienced it, and I have witnessed it many times. And that is what the Bible promises."

The chaplain paused for a moment to gather his thoughts. Then he said, "A great Christian philosopher once pointed out that all persons, whether they choose to acknowledge it or not, are in relationship to God, to their Creator. Each of us has a relationship with God which defines our identity as a self, as a person. And our relationship with God defines all of our other relationships, as well. Who you are as a person, and how you live your life in this world, are defined by your relationship with God. And this philosopher said the fundamental problem we have as human beings, is that we are unwilling to be the selves that we really are. We are unwilling to *be* selves related to God. And we are unwilling to be selves related to other people, places, things and situations God has placed in our lives. In other words, our problem as human beings is our reluctance to play the cards we have been dealt, to pick up the pieces and choose to live our lives in each moment as gifts of God."

"Angela, you can do that," The chaplain said. "It will not be easy. But if you ask, God will help you."

Angela's story might have ended differently, as it does in so many lives where suicide is considered. She could have been back in the hospital a few months later. Or her grieving parents could have watched her coffin lowered, as Angela had watched Tony's. But that is not how Angela's story turned out. Angela never again attempted suicide, and never again returned to a psychiatric hospital. And she did discover what she believed was God's purpose for her life, as she experienced the Psalmist's words:

"Though I walk in the midst of trouble, you preserve my life." (Psalm 138:7a *NIV*)

Phase III
The Grace to Embrace Reality

Chapter 8
The Road To Recovery Is
Paved With Moments of Grace

"Not only so, but we also rejoice in our sufferings, because we know that suffering produces perseverance; perseverance, character; and character, hope. And hope does not disappoint us, because God has poured out his love into our hearts by the Holy Spirit, whom he has given us."
(Romans 5:3-5 NIV)

Acceptance

As suggested throughout the previous chapters, grief is a normal response to a significant loss. The journey of grief can be a pathway to healing. But whether healing takes place or not depends a great deal on the choices we make along the way. The journey of grief is not a comfortable ride on an aircraft in which, once we are in transit, we have no responsibility until it is time to disembark. The journey of grief is more like a marathon over treacherous terrain. It requires personal commitment, great effort, and the willingness to experience pain. It requires strategy, pacing, endurance, and determination to reach the goal.

Unlike a marathon, however, we do not have to rely entirely upon ourselves in order to complete this pilgrimage. The rules of the journey of grief allow and encourage us to ask for and to receive assistance. *The failure to ask for help probably is the single greatest reason people get bogged down along the way.* There are professionals, friends, and loved ones who desire to assist us, if only we are willing to ask.

And above all, if we have eyes of faith, we can see that God continually is reaching out to help us, and to guide us through our dark valleys to a place of healing.

It has been said that time heals all things. That just is not so. Many people get stuck in one or more of the stages of grief, and never reach acceptance. For people of faith, a more accurate way to understand how healing comes about is, "God will heal us in God's time, if we are willing to live in reality and to walk in faith." Our responsibility on the journey of grief is to find that willingness so that we might, with God's help, experience the grace to embrace the changed reality of our lives.

THE GIFT OF ACCEPTANCE

The seasons of grief are times for emotional and spiritual work. But acceptance does not come about through our efforts alone. It is a gift of grace, whether or not we acknowledge it as such. During our time of grief, God is working on our behalf, every step of the way. Acceptance is the goal of our journey, but we do not find it. It finds us, when, in God's time, we are ready for it.

We know we have reached acceptance when we are no longer in denial, no longer trying to run away, no longer playing the victim role. Acceptance means we have stopped questioning God's goodness, and have begun to trust God's love for us. And acceptance is the end of blaming, the termination of feelings of despair, and the absence of the impulse to give up.

There is a life-and-death difference between the journey of grief which ends in depression, and the one that leads to acceptance. Depression is resignation without tranquility, without the willingness to adapt, without hope and without confidence in God. Acceptance is surrender with serenity, accompanied by the willingness to change. And acceptance is hope-filled anticipation, with trust in God's comfort and care.

THE WILLINGNESS TO LET GO

In order for acceptance to be real, it must be a letting go of the past and of the persons, things, or circumstances we have lost. If we fail to let go, we are at risk of becoming the psychological equivalent of Lot's wife. We are in danger of becoming emotionally frozen. And over time, we may lose our ability to cope with the present and to engage the future.

But *while acceptance involves releasing, it does not mean forgetting.* If we forget, we cannot learn life's lessons. A divorce, for example, contains lessons about life which inform the present and the future. And a marriage usually is a storehouse of memories which have shaped both spouses and could be important to children, relatives and friends. If that is the case, then letting go should not mean the destruction of those memories. Rather, what is called for is the grateful acknowledgement of the blessings of the past, free of imprisonment to what is no more.

We disrespect the past when we remain burdened with regrets on the one hand, or we continue to obsess over its passing, on the other. When we know acceptance, we no longer feel that we must rewrite the past. We trust that God can and will mysteriously bring good out of what has been. And we are free to get on with the task of living and of creating the story of our future.

Similarly, when our loved ones have died, we do not reach acceptance until we are willing to let go. But letting go does not mean we are supposed to forget those who have been dear to us. The wonderful moments we shared with them are treasures which never can be taken away from us. Nor does releasing the past mean the end of our love. If we truly love another, that love does not end with death. It is important to find a place in our hearts where those who have shared our journey can remain, and where they always will be loved and honored.

If we forget the past, we fail to respect it. But if we cling too much to what has been, we may be in danger of dishonoring it even more. It is important to remember that those who genuinely have loved us would not want us to condemn ourselves to a lifetime of sorrow. When a personal tragedy happens, we may, for a time, feel it would be wrong to feel happiness ever again. Acceptance means we have reached the point on our journey where we again can feel the joy God desires to bestow upon us. And to accept that happiness is not a failure to honor the past. It is to honor, in a profound way, those who are no longer with us, and their unending wishes for us to be happy, to know true joy.

THE WILLINGNESS TO CHANGE

But acceptance is more than the willingness to release the past. It also is about the willingness to change. A life-changing loss brings with it the need for *practical* alterations. These alterations require realistic actions. In the early stages of grief, it is usually best for us to make only minor changes in our daily lives. Familiar routines and our networks of family and friends can bring us great comfort, and should be disturbed as little as possible. For that reason, many grief counselors recommend that we should wait a year after a loss before making a major change, such as a long-distance residential move.

But over time, the practical changes we need to make usually become clear to us. The nature of these, of course, depends upon individual circumstances and on the kinds of personal tragedies experienced. Persons losing the use of a limb in an accident or in combat, for example, may need to make changes in their living environments and to develop new skills for managing the activities of daily living. Parents of teen-age children who have had an onset of mental illness may need to alter their work schedules in order to provide twenty-four hours a day monitoring. A young stay-at-home wife may need to find a job, after her husband has betrayed and abandoned her. And a widow may need to move closer to relatives, or to find a roommate.

While these are only examples of possibilities, they illustrate the truth that, when it comes to change, one size does *not* fit all. One clear indication that we have reached at least a degree of acceptance, is our willingness to identify the specific practical changes necessary for our particular journeys. And of course, acceptance means that this recognition is followed by the development of realistic plans, which, in turn, are followed by necessary actions.

But practical matters are not the only things requiring change. *Every personal tragedy is an opportunity to grow spiritually.* The Apostle Paul found that suffering is capable of producing perseverance, then character, and then hope. Acceptance means we are willing for God to help us mature in our faith.

To live in acceptance means we are open to learn even the most difficult lessons from our experiences. The time of acceptance is a time for letting go of old attitudes and the cultivation of new ones. Our sufferings can help us develop a better understanding of the way life is, and of the mystery of God's care for us. And they can lead us to a greater awareness of the suffering of others, and thereby open avenues of service to God and neighbor.

GOD'S COMFORT AND CARE

Acceptance also is characterized by the desire to be healed and the willingness to trust the Healer. The healings of Jesus recorded in the Gospels underscore the importance of the petitioners' faith. In order for healing to occur, typically it was necessary for people to want and ask for healing. They also had to trust that Jesus could and would heal them.

Our healing may not come to us as suddenly as those in the Bible. Physical healing sometimes takes a long time. So does spiritual healing. But whether recovery from our grieving occurs quickly or over an extended period, the desire to be healed, and the willingness to trust in God's comfort and care, remain prerequisites.

The grace of God that comforts, sustains, and transforms us as people of faith, comes to us when we open our hearts to receive it. We may find ourselves finally ready to accept this grace only when we have *hit bottom*, feel defeated, have nowhere else to turn, and cry out to God for help. But willingness also may come to us in less dramatic moments, especially when we, as people of faith, are in the midst of praying, reading and studying the Scriptures, attending worship, or participating in the sacred rituals of our various traditions. These are tried and true activities that help us to open ourselves to God. It is no accident that these activities are sometimes called *means of grace.*

God also works grace in us in other mysterious ways. Sometimes it happens in a moment of sudden illumination, when a thought presses upon us, one we instinctively know comes from God. Sometimes it happens when we are struck by a demonstration of the majesty and beauty of God's Creation and feel a warm peace wash over us. And at other times it happens because we encounter another human being whose presence, words, and actions become the channel through which God speaks to us. Such times are *moments of grace,* and through them God works healing in us.

When we are on the journey of grief, it is important to pay attention, to notice, and to listen for God to speak, comfort, and guide. For persons of faith, there are no coincidences in life. God is at work in all things.

David

When Rachel arrived home from the doctor that day, having been given the diagnosis of cancer and a prognosis of a year to live, her husband David saw the evidence of shock, fear, and sorrow on her face. He tried to comfort and assure her, as best he could, but it was difficult to transcend his own feeling that he could not possibly deal with this.

Those who knew Rachel thought of her as wonderful, even irreplaceable in their lives. The nursing staff at the hospital appreciated her for her kind and wise management style. Her personal friends, and her friends at church, experienced her as a compassionate spiritual presence. David knew both sets of extended family loved Rachel, and would be devastated by her passing. Yet he knew that all of these people would be able to grieve for a while, and then get their lives back to normal.

But Rachel was *his* soul-mate, the love of his *life*. How could he watch her suffer and die? How could he survive such a great loss? How could life ever be normal for him again? And most of all, David wondered, how could he possibly stand to experience the pain of his three children, as they lost the mother who had nurtured them, upon whom they were dependent every day, and whom they adored? It was all too horrible to contemplate.

Three years after Rachel's death, David walked to the podium as the speaker at a large Interfaith Breakfast as the speaker. Because of the recommendation of his own pastor, David had been invited that morning by the President of the citywide Interfaith Counsel to talk about how faith had sustained and assisted him through his personal tragedy. As he reflected on the experience of Rachel's death, he felt completely undeserving of being held up as an example of strong faith in the midst of difficulty. He was painfully aware of the weakness of his personal faith, and of those times when he was tempted to abandon his faith altogether along the way. That is why he originally had declined the invitation to speak.

Upon reflection, however, it dawned on David that the speech was not about what he had done. It was not about his personal struggle and triumph. It was about what *God* had done to care for him along the way. David knew the real story of his life the past three years was that God had given him what he needed, in the midst of his own weakness and personal despair, at each critical stage of his dealing with the tragic change in his family. That is why David called the Council President back and agreed to be the speaker. And that is why he titled his speech: "The Road to Recovery is Paved with Moments of Grace."

When she was first diagnosed, the doctors had given Rachel a year to live. She survived almost eighteen months. David had thought at first it was his job to help Rachel through those difficult times. He found instead that it was *Rachel's* strength and courage which had sustained *him* during those terribly difficult months.

David encouraged Rachel to quit work. He told her to take care of herself. While he was away at work and the children were at school, he wanted her to spend more time doing the things she enjoyed. But Rachel chose to keep on working. The hospital was where she felt normal and useful, and working had the added benefit of keeping her health insurance in place so that she would not become a financial burden to her family.

Rachel did arrange with the Vice-President of Nursing to go home most afternoons in time to be with her children. And the family spent many weekends at their second home in the mountains together, until Rachel became too sick to go there. Her sickness was made greater because she chose an experimental form of chemotherapy in a long-shot effort to find a cure. She knew it probably would not work, and it would make her physically miserable. But if there were any chance at all that she could beat the odds, it was worth a try. Thinking about her three girls was all the motivation she needed.

Rachel's determination to live her life with courage as a terminally ill person was nothing short of amazing, and David was made stronger by it. "We all are going to die," she would say. "The important thing for any of us is to decide what we are going to do with the time we have left."

Rachel's situation, and those words, increased David's awareness of his own mortality. It made him think more seriously than ever before about what was truly important to him. Rachel's words were a moment of grace for David, a moment when he knew that God was speaking to him about his own life.

David was strengthened, perhaps more than by any other events in those final eighteen months with Rachel, by their "happy moments." One night, Rachel and David were about to settle down when Rachel asked David, "What was your happy moment today?"

The question took David completely by surprise. His consciousness had been so saturated by fear and anguish over the weeks since learning of Rachel's condition, that he found it difficult at first to imagine there had been any happy moments in any recent days.

"My happy moment today," Rachel volunteered, "was when I looked out the kitchen window and saw two hummingbirds drinking from our feeder. What was your happy moment?"

David hesitated. He was not sure he could come up with anything. But then he remembered something. "I guess my happy moment was when I was driving to work this morning. They played one of our songs. It made me remember some of the wonderful times we have shared together." David did not tell Rachel the memories had caused his eyes to fill with tears. But upon reflection, it was, he thought, as close to a happy moment as he could find that day.

After that, Rachel and David agreed to create a nighttime ritual in which each of them would name a happy moment of the day. David was amazed at the way Rachel could be miserable from her treatments and, in the later stages, the ravages of her disease, and still find a happy moment. Sometimes it was in the form of an inspirational e-mail one of her friends had sent her. Sometimes it was a conversation with one of the girls about something happening at school. Sometimes it was the sharing of a sunset with David, or a moment of quiet intimacy with him. Not a day went by that Rachel could not identify her happy moment.

David also was surprised that as the weeks passed he could identify more easily his own happy moments. He began to anticipate and recognize such moments when they happened, even during the darkest of days. He realized that before Rachel's diagnosis he had missed noticing and appreciating the many little blessings each day held. Now he not only recognized these moments, but he also had come to understand them as daily gifts from God. When recognized, they provided reassurance that God was with him and with his family in the midst of this terrible thing happening to them. These were significant moments of grace. They made possible strength and endurance through the awful times.

David shared all these things with the more than five hundred persons gathered that morning. He also told them about the morning he and Rachel had received the terrible news about the experimental treatments. They had failed to halt the growth of the tumors. Hospice would need to be called in, as the time was growing short.

On that gloomy Saturday morning, Rachel and David were drinking coffee silently at the breakfast table, when David's father paid them an unexpected visit. David's father was a reserved man, never one to demonstrate affection. His family contribution through the years had been that of a hard-working provider who lived a quiet life of personal integrity. David did not remember a time when his father ever had said he loved him, or had offered him anything more affectionate than a handshake. But this morning was different.

David's father spoke first to Rachel. He told her how sorry he was that she was going through all of this. He then told both of them about the darkest moment of his own life. His first daughter, David's younger sister, appeared healthy when she was born. But then she began to turn blue. The physicians discovered that the infant's internal organs had not developed properly. After three days, she died. David had known about his baby sister's death, but this was the first time he ever had heard his father speak of it. It was, David's father said, the most painful moment of his life.

David's grandfather, who attended the infant's funeral, had the reputation of being even less likely than David's father to express emotion or affection. But David's father now described how, at the graveside, as they were burying the baby, David's grandfather placed his arm around the grieving father and told him, for the first time, that he loved him.

After telling Rachel and David about this important event in his own life, David's father went to each of them, in turn. He placed his arms around them, and gave each of them a big hug, while telling them he loved them. Without saying more, he left. Rachel and David looked at each other in amazement. They were deeply moved. Both of them knew what their "happy moment" would be for that day.

A week later, David's father dropped dead of a heart attack. It was not entirely a surprise. David's father had survived quadruple bypass surgery a few years earlier. But Rachel and David could not help but wonder if the old gentleman somehow had felt a premonition of what was to come, the day he had uttered those simple but incredibly powerful words, and had given them those memorable hugs.

When he learned of his father's death, David knew he would be burying a father and a wife in the same year. In a strange way, the funeral of his father provided a kind of preparation for Rachel's imminent death. The worship service turned out to be a joyful celebration of his father's life. The pastor reminded those gathered of the promises of God. The children and grandchildren took turns speaking of their love and admiration for this quiet, remarkable gentleman.

David knew Rachel's death would be more difficult for him by far than the death of his father. Yet as he faced Rachel's last weeks, the shared memories along with the faith and hope of the family for his father's transition to Heaven gave him a quiet assurance he had not known before.

When Rachel finally succumbed to her disease, there was a large outpouring of sympathy and concern from friends and family. David was overwhelmed with the greatest sense of loss he had ever known. But after watching the love of his life experience pain, grow weak, and fade away during those last few weeks, David also experienced relief.

For a while, David felt guilty about his sense of relief. He also felt guilty because, toward the end, he had prayed for God to take Rachel. But upon reflection, David realized that he did not need to feel guilty. He had not prayed for her death for any selfish reason. Those were the prayers of a man who loved Rachel and did not want her to suffer.

The memorial service for Rachel packed the church to overflowing. While the pastor was speaking, something he said struck home to David. Looking directly at the family, he said to the husband, the children and other relatives, "Feel your grief. Let it happen. And as you permit your sorrow to have its time, remember that 'weeping tarries for the night, but joy comes in the morning light.'" And then the minister recalled a conversation with Rachel, in which Rachel said she had found comfort in a verse from a hymn which helped her through her time of trial: "When through the deep waters I cause you to go, the rivers of sorrow will not overflow."

David had heard these words from Rachel's lips several times over the past eighteen months. And as the pastor said them, the grieving husband felt certain he could hear Rachel saying them once again. They were words meant for him.

Rachel had spent considerable time, during the final year of her life, writing letters and buying presents. She wrote one letter and bought one present for each of her children for each birthday through the age of twenty-one. She attempted to imagine each child at the age of a particular birthday, to buy an age-appropriate gift, and to offer in the letter some good motherly advice. David was given the responsibility to make sure these gifts and letters were a part of each birthday celebration. After three years and nine such birthdays, David continued to be impressed with how the children looked forward to those gifts and letters. Rather than creating melancholy on those occasions, as David had feared they would, they generated excitement and emotional warmth.

Rachel also had written one letter to David. He obediently waited to open it until the one-year anniversary of her death. In that letter, Rachel told him she knew God had brought them together and blessed them with a wonderful marriage and three beautiful daughters. She told him how much she loved him, and she knew he missed her terribly, and that there would never be another who could replace her in his heart. But she also told him she knew that he needed a wife and the girls needed a mother. She asked him to forgive her for not being able to be that wife and mother any more. And she encouraged him to let God lead him to find someone who would appreciate him as the great husband, father, and human being he was, and who would love and care for the girls as if they were her own. David was not sure he could ever allow himself to fall in love again. But by now, three years later, he had remarried and was making a new life with a very special woman. He had met her while attending a support group for people whose spouses had died.

As he told his personal story on that morning, David noted that at each juncture, at each turning point, God had provided what David needed in order to get through the excruciatingly tough times, and to find the life God intended for him after the terrible tragedy of losing Rachel.

"Throughout it all," David said, "I have grown in my capacity to feel the lows and the highs of life, to observe the small miracles present in our lives every day, and to empathize with the suffering and the joys of others. And I have become convinced in my own faith that God wants us to face reality, no matter how difficult it is to do so. He wants us to accept our losses in life, and be willing to struggle through them. When we deny them, or run from them, or just stop trying in the face of them, we not only become dysfunctional as human beings in dealing with our problems. We also cut ourselves off from the spiritual growth God wants to work in us."

"Studies in the stages of grief have shown it is when one reaches the stage of acceptance, that one finally finds some peace. It comes when reality not only is faced, but when it is embraced. It happens when one makes one's peace with the inevitable. But for a person of faith, I believe there is more."

"Facing and accepting reality is more than facing and embracing the bad things that happen to us. Reality includes God's love for us. Reality includes God's presence with us in our suffering, and God's compassion toward us. Reality is God putting God's arm around us, and hugging us, and telling us God too has suffered, and God loves us more than we can imagine."

"The road to recovery is paved with moments of grace. Reality includes those moments of transparency when we catch glimpses, in the midst of our sorrows and everyday struggles, that God is with us, God is for us, and God will never abandon us. To anyone facing a terrible loss today, my advice is to use your spiritual eyes and see *all* of reality. Moments of grace happen every day."

Chapter 9
Transforming Your Season of Grieving into a Lifetime of Caring

"But Joseph said to them, 'Don't be afraid. Am I in the place of God? You intended to harm me, but God intended it for good to accomplish what is now being done, the saving of many lives'." (Gen. 50:20 NIV)

Calling

The gift of acceptance may come rather suddenly and dramatically for some. But for most of us, it comes slowly, in bits and pieces over time. Our journeys are not traveled in straight lines. We wander from one stage of grief to another, meandering back and forth, and occasionally going in circles. At some point, if we are fortunate, we realize we have arrived at our destination. We may not know exactly when it happened or how we got there. But we have come to experience an inner peace we once believed was impossible to know again.

One of the reasons our journeys are so difficult and slow is that we are not at all sure we want to reach acceptance. Even when we are willing to be free of our bitterness and despair, we tend to doubt we ever will come to terms with the terrible things which have happened. We struggle with the notion that it would be wrong to accept them. And we find it difficult to believe anything good could come from them.

Despite such struggles, if we finally do come to know acceptance, it may be because we have experienced a calling in the midst of our grief. And that calling has transformed us from victims of terrible events to agents of change. Such life-altering calls generally come about in one of two ways. The first involves the transformation of anger into a passion for righting the wrongs our personal tragedies have made known to us. The second way is the transformation of our personal sorrow into empathy for those whose agony is similar to our own.

In the former case, passion usually comes first, followed by empathy. In the latter, empathy usually comes first, followed by passion. In both cases, the results are similar. We feel called to the work of preventing or alleviating the suffering of others. And when we respond, we set out to make the world a better place. Perhaps unknowingly, we also open ourselves to receive God's healing for our own emotional wounds.

FROM ANGER TO PASSION

As we discussed in Chapter 6, anger can be a dangerous emotion. Both for our sakes and for the sakes of others, we need to be free from the power bitterness and resentments have over us. But that does not mean we should banish all feelings of anger on our road to recovery. *Anger over tragedies caused by human sin and perversity, and over unnecessary suffering due to human ignorance, callousness or neglect, can lead to actions which give meaning to our suffering.*

With appropriate intervention, many tragic events can be prevented. And if they cannot be prevented, at least the suffering they produce can be alleviated. We may not be able to respond directly to all the problems and sufferings of the world. But our indignation over a particular form of human suffering can be an indicator of a problem God is laying on our hearts for a reason.

In the book of Exodus, we learn that Moses angrily killed an Egyptian who was beating a Hebrew slave. As a result, Moses fled his privileged life in the household of Pharaoh to the land of

Midian, where he lived in exile for decades. But the story makes it clear that the plight of his Hebrew brothers and sisters in Egypt, which continued to worsen, weighed heavily on Moses' heart. It is reasonable to assume that his initial anger over the oppression of the Egyptians never fully left him.

In a burning bush spiritual experience, Moses heard God's call to return to Egypt. It was a mission which would expose him to great personal danger. Moses answered the call. And the rest, as we say, is history. A journey which began as anger at the treatment of a Hebrew brother, resulted in the loss of a privileged life and important relationships. But later, that anger and personal tragedy became a calling to free an entire people from the suffering of slavery, and to change the course of human events.

In our own time, there are many examples of people who have channeled the righteous anger born of personal suffering into passionate advocacy. One thinks, for example, of the outraged mother of a child killed by a drunk driver who became active in MADD (Mothers Against Drunk Driving) and an advocate in her state for creative sentencing of persons convicted of driving while intoxicated.

Or one remembers the wife who was refused treatment at a psychiatric facility because she did not meet the criteria for admission. Within hours of being turned away, she committed suicide. Her incensed husband worked to change the wording of commitment laws in his state, so that persons with symptoms similar to those of his wife would be deemed to meet the criteria for admission. Through the actions of such people, the suffering of others often is alleviated or prevented altogether.

FROM SORROW TO EMPATHY

The other avenue, which often results in a calling to become an agent of change, is the transformation of sorrow into empathy. *Because we know first-hand what our own suffering is like, we can empathize with the emotional pain of others in similar circumstances.* This can be a natural path for those of us whose sadness is so great that we are tempted to despair. Instead of letting ourselves lose hope, we identify with the suffering of others, particularly those going through similar tragic situations.

When we empathize with others, we walk in their shoes. We are able to communicate our identification with their feelings in nonverbal ways. And when we do speak, we are able to connect with them at a profound level, because we genuinely do feel their pain.

When we empathize with the suffering of others, their sense of isolation is overcome. Their burdens are made lighter, because they no longer feel they must bear them alone. That is one of the reasons support groups consisting of people who have experienced similar losses are so effective in helping people heal. When members share their similar stories with each another, the fellowship of their suffering is a source of courage, strength and hope.

Whenever our feelings of empathy are strong, we may be receiving a call to serve others. Empathy can give us the insight and compassion to work for much-needed change. Most of us know or are aware of people who have allowed their personal agony to be transformed through empathy into service and advocacy. For example, we may know someone who decided to enter a medical career after dealing with an injury or illness in the family. Or we may have learned from a television program about a wife who became an advocate for funding research to find a cure for a disease that afflicted her husband. There are many such examples.

Some extraordinary people have become famous because of their efforts on behalf of their causes. But most of those who have their grief transformed into a calling are ordinary people who will receive little or no recognition for their efforts. They use their talents and skills, as best they can, to help bring about change. It is important to remember that a calling is not always about a grandiose cause. It may be as simple as taking meals to the sick or offering to transport others to doctor appointments.

Most of us do not answer a call in order to receive recognition, but because we desire for the suffering of a loved one not to have been in vain. We want it to mean something. And many of us have found that the best way for this to happen is to find ways for our personal losses to help others.

FROM EVIL TO GOOD

Sometimes, however, things happen that are so very horrific that it is difficult to see how anything constructive can come from them. This may seem especially true when tragic events are the result of the evil actions of cruel and violent people. Nevertheless, when the suffering of those touched by such events becomes a calling, victims can become God's instruments for transforming evil into good. The Biblical stories of Esther and Joseph dramatically illustrate this possibility.

Esther was a Jewish orphan during the time when the Jews were suffering in captivity and exile in Persia. Because of her natural beauty, she was selected by a representative of the king and forced to become a member of the king's harem. In order to survive in that role, she concealed her ethnic identity. The king was impressed with Esther and soon chose her to be his queen.

Later, at the instigation of one of his chief nobles, the king allowed his authority to be used to order the annihilation of the Jewish people. When Esther learned of this, she risked her life by revealing her identity to the king, and begged him to intercede on behalf of her people. The king did so, the Jews were spared, and the Jewish annual feast of Purim was instituted.

In the story of Joseph in the book of Genesis, the boy with the coat of many colors was the victim of his brothers' jealousy and hatred. They attacked him and intended to kill him. But due to the intervention of one of the brothers, he was sold into slavery instead.

Many years later, Joseph rose in the ranks of Pharaoh's palace to the position of overseer of the storehouses of grain. When his brothers came to Egypt during a famine to ask for food, they were brought before him. The brothers did not recognize Joseph. But he recognized them. When he finally revealed himself to them, they were afraid he would kill them out of revenge. But Joseph forgave them. He told them their actions were intended to do evil, but God had intended them for good. With those words, Joseph expressed a statement of faith that became a central theme in the Judaeo-Christian tradition: *God is able to transform the evil of human beings into God's good work.* For Christians, the greatest symbol of this faith is the crucifixion of Jesus.

When we have come to know the inward change which occurs in acceptance, we may find it accompanied by a particular calling. Having experienced the grace to let go of the past, to face the future, and to know serenity, we are able to transcend our own difficulties and to see the suffering of others as a sign of what God would have us to do now.

But as we have seen, a calling also may come to us even as we continue to struggle in the midst of anger and sorrow. As our anger turns into passion and our sorrow is transformed into empathy, we may feel a persistent urge to become agents of change. When we answer that call, a strange thing is likely to happen to us. At some point along the way, while we are engaged in our mission, our inner agony frequently will be replaced by an inner peace. And this will be so, even if we remain engaged in an outwardly fierce struggle.

As people of faith, regardless of when and how it comes to us, if we answer our calling and commit our lives to it, we are able to experience the mysterious activity of our God transforming the evil that has come upon us into God's good and loving work.

Nancy

It was the third day of the trial when Nancy was called to the stand to testify. That day was the first time, since she had identified the two men in a lineup eighteen months ago, she had come face to face with either of them. Only one of them sat with his attorney at the defense table. The other would appear later as a witness for the prosecution. As she glanced at him, Nancy noticed that the accused had a neatly trimmed haircut and was dressed in a dark blue suit. She could still recognize him, but his appearance had changed dramatically from the unkempt wild-eyed man she remembered. At the sight of him, Nancy had to fight back the desire to run out of the courtroom and as far away as possible from this terrible person.

Under the guidance of the prosecutor, Nancy told the court her story of the night in question. The evening had begun as so many other pleasant ones had in their family home and quiet neighborhood. Nancy, her husband Carl, and their three-year old daughter Keri, had finished dinner. After the dishes were done, and Keri had been put to bed upstairs, Carl and Nancy settled down to watch television in the family room. Around eight-thirty, the doorbell rang. Thinking it probably was a neighbor friend who frequently would drop by in the evenings, Nancy went to the door and began to open it. Suddenly, two men dressed in dark clothes knocked her backward as they pushed open the door. One of them grabbed Nancy. She screamed. Carl got up to see what was happening. He was confronted by a young man with a gun who ordered him to sit back down. The two men held the couple at gunpoint until Carl was tied up. Then they forced him to watch as they ripped off Nancy's clothes and raped her time after time.

As Nancy described the terror of her ordeal, several persons in the courtroom and on the jury visibly were shaken. Nancy told how she attempted to fight back at first. When they threatened to kill Carl if she did not comply, she realized she needed to stop struggling. She finally did so, but not before she had dug her fingernails deeply into the man who now sat before her in the courtroom.

The rapists spent several hours, taking turns assaulting her. Then they casually took a break and raided the refrigerator. They found a couple of bottles of wine and began to drink them. As the kitchen was open to the family room, they were able to watch their two victims. Nancy lay on the floor, pretending to be unconscious. She suddenly jumped up, ran to Carl, and attempted to untie him. The man now on trial saw her. Instead of retrieving his gun from the kitchen counter where he had laid it, he grabbed a butcher knife from the rack, ran over to Nancy, pulled her head back, and slit her throat. She collapsed to the floor and lost consciousness.

Nancy could not provide direct testimony for what happened next. But she had been told about it later, and had been over it in her mind many times. After the invader slit her throat, he turned to Carl, who was still tied up and defenseless, and also slit his throat. Carl died almost instantly. The two men then went through the house, looking for valuables. They found some change in a jar in the master bedroom closet. They took some of Nancy's costume jewelry. They never found her expensive jewelry. But they did find Carl and Nancy's daughter Keri. They put tape over Keri's mouth. They wrapped her in a blanket, and took her with them as they left the house near midnight.

A neighbor walking his dog saw the two men struggling to carry a bundle while running to a car. He watched as they loaded it in the back seat of the vehicle and sped away. Alarmed, he dialed 911 on his cell phone and reported the incident. When the police arrived, they discovered that, miraculously, Nancy still had a pulse. An ambulance arrived a few minutes later, and she was transported to the community hospital.

Nancy almost died that night. She lost a lot of blood. It was feared her internal organs would shut down. It was several days before the physicians were confident she would make it, and many weeks before her physical recovery was complete. The emotional recovery would be another matter.

During the first few days after the attack, the entire community rallied around in support of the victims. People were terrified. They found it difficult to imagine such a thing could happen in what they had believed to be a safe neighborhood. They organized a massive effort to find little Keri. They systematically searched the local parks, vacant lots, and several wooded sections on the outskirts of town. They posted pictures of Keri on light poles and in store windows. Three television stations carried photos of the three-year-old and asked for the public's assistance. The faith communities set in motion candlelight vigils and prayer chains. But Keri could not be found.

The investigation of the crime focused immediately on information provided by the neighbor who had called the police. He managed to remember part of a license plate identification, and to describe the car. When the police ran the possible plates, one match turned out to be a car registered to a felon who previously had been convicted of armed robbery and rape. Only six weeks before the assault on Nancy's home, this man had been released from prison, even though he had been scheduled to serve many more years. The convict had been set free early, because the prosecutor who had convicted him had committed prosecutorial misconduct in an unrelated trial. As a result of the misconduct case, eight persons previously convicted in separate cases were released pending retrials.

The evidence against the accused was overwhelming. His partner in crime was a former cellmate with a record of breaking and entering to support a drug habit. This second attacker reached a plea agreement in which the death penalty was taken off the table in his case, in return for his full confession, for his testimony against the accused, and for information leading to the recovery of Keri's remains. After the agreement was signed, he led authorities to the location of a shallow grave in a field. Two days later, the community turned out in large numbers for Keri's funeral, to express their sympathy to the victims and their outrage at the perpetrators.

When the second attacker took the stand, he testified he and the accused had seen Nancy at the grocery store that day. They followed her home, determined to come back later with the intent of raping her. After he confirmed Nancy's version of the events of the evening, and testified it was the accused who personally had murdered the father and child, the forensic evidence was presented. It dramatically supported the testimony that the two men had been in the house where the crime took place. DNA tests verified that the skin scrapings under Nancy's fingernails belonged to the accused.

The jury took less than four hours to return a verdict of guilty. A day later, after the penalty hearing, the jury recommended the death penalty. The judge formalized their recommendation by sentencing the attacker to death by lethal injection.

Nancy had hoped when the trial was over she would feel some closure. She was not sure what that would feel like, but she had heard others speak of it. She did feel a little safer. She found she could sleep through an entire night without waking up in fear, now that the two men were safely behind bars to stay. She had hoped the results of the trial also would bring some kind of inward satisfaction that would allow her to feel less pain about all that had happened. But that did not happen.

As Nancy soon realized, the failure to experience the healing she longed for had nothing to do with the fact that it would take many years before the sentence was carried out. She now understood that even if the execution of the man who had raped her and murdered her child and husband were to take place immediately, the relief for which she was desperately longing would not come. It would not come because it would not bring back Keri and Carl. Nothing would ever be the same again.

Nancy had spent much of the year leading up to the trial filled with rage toward those two men. After the trial, her anger settled into a bitter resentment accompanied by depression. She had read somewhere that there are stages to grieving, and that people eventually are supposed to reach a state of acceptance. She doubted that would be possible for her. She also was under the impression that some people get stuck in their anger and depression and never reach acceptance. She thought she might be one of those people. She felt she could never *accept* the unimaginable things which happened to her and her loved ones.

She remembered having been taught as a child, that God works in all things for good. But she could not believe any good could come out of such a horror. She realized she was not just angry with those evil men. As many other victims of unspeakable acts, she was deeply and profoundly angry with God for not intervening, for allowing such terrible things to happen. Nancy reasoned, "If our faith cannot provide protection from unspeakable evil, then what good is it?".

As she reflected on these things, she decided she was not going to believe in God any more. "Believing in nothing was better than believing in God," she told herself. Some people might have stuck with that decision for a lifetime. But, for Nancy, it only lasted until her next visit to the cemetery.

When Nancy knelt by the graves of her husband and daughter, she found herself unable to resist the urge to turn once more to God. She was not looking for answers that day to the mystery of evil in the world, or why terrible things happen to people completely out of proportion to any wrong they have ever done. She knew in her heart, after what she had been through, that no explanation ever could be adequate. But she also knew she could not give up on God, because she needed God that morning. She could not face the future without Carl and Keri, without help from a Power greater than herself.

What Nancy was seeking that morning was some comfort and

assurance. She wanted to believe Carl and Keri were with God and each other, and that they were in a wonderful place where evil could no longer touch them. She wanted God to comfort her and assure her she would one day be with them again, and they all would be happy. And she wanted to believe, in the meantime, it was possible for her to find some semblance of happiness once more in her own life.

Nancy realized at the cemetery that the anger and resentment she still harbored toward the attackers was eating her up inside. She did not want to forgive them, and she did not want God to forgive them. "They should never be forgiven," she thought. She wanted them to rot in hell. But, now that the trial was over, she also longed to be free of the evil that had fallen upon her family. She realized that as long as she was consumed with hatred toward her attackers, their evil still had power over her, as it had the night they held her down and raped her. As long as she feared and hated them, she was still their victim.

Reluctantly, she found herself praying for God to help her find enough forgiveness to release her from the hatred and resentment which was imprisoning her. And she prayed God would move the mountain of her despair and give her hope and spiritual peace again.

She did not feel much confidence that God would answer her prayers.

Her lack of faith was much greater than the little bit of faith remaining in her heart. But she remembered Jesus' saying that even if someone's faith is only the size of a tiny seed, it could still move mountains. In the midst of her prayers, Nancy felt a sudden urge to stand up and look around the cemetery.

As she surveyed the burial sites stretching in all directions, she became curiously aware of many crosses. The crosses came in various shapes, styles and sizes. And as she observed them, she thought about Jesus' suffering and dying on the cross. At that moment, the realization that God had not intervened to save Jesus from an awful death pressed itself on her mind. She had believed, as long as she could remember, that Jesus had died for our sins. But for the first time, she now began to understand what he had gone through on that cross. And she remembered and was comforted by the words he had cried out, "My God, My God, Why have you forsaken me?". Jesus must have felt that day exactly as she was feeling – God-forsaken.

It occurred to Nancy, as she reflected on those crosses at the cemetery, that she had been going through the season of her own personal Black Friday. She left the graves that day with a spark of hope in her heart for a new season, the season of the resurrection of her own spirit. She wanted again to take charge of her life. She wanted the stone to be rolled away and to be able to come out of the tomb of her own despair. It had become clear to her that there must be a reason why she had not died along with her husband and daughter. The only thing she could come up with was, there must be something she was supposed to do with her life, so that evil would not have the last word.

The spiritual resurrection Nancy hoped for did not come through some dramatic religious insight or experience. It came a few days after her latest visit to the cemetery, in the most mundane of ways. She was watching one of the talk shows on television. The topic of "everyday heroes" grabbed her attention. This was a program about people who had been through personal suffering, and who had found in that suffering a calling to service. Nancy watched and listened carefully.

One of the everyday heroes was a man who, as a young boy, had been sexually abused by a priest. This man had joined with other victims to help bring about important reforms to assure that such priests were no longer able to hide behind the curtain of secrecy and continue their pedophilic ways. Another person on the show was a woman who had struggled through many years with her mentally ill son's strange and sometimes violent behaviors. She had found her calling as an organizer of family support groups, and as an advocate for better mental health treatment and services. Still another was a young woman, who was HIV positive. She had dedicated herself to preventive education and to advocating for more funding for research to improve treatment and eventually to find a cure for the disease.

A virtual parade of such heroes appeared on the program. Nancy learned that many of the important laws passed in various states and nationally over the past few decades were the result of someone turning personal tragedy into something good. Some of the heroes faced very different troubles from Nancy's horrendous experience. Several had been the victims of misfortune, and of unintentional, though in some cases preventable, events. These persons had not been the victims of cruel and violent evil at the hands of others who wanted to do them harm. In comparison, Nancy's experience felt like it was in a class by itself.

Yet there also were people on the program whose experiences were similar to her own. They also had been victims of violent crimes. One man, for example, had been severely disabled when he was shot during a convenience store robbery. Another ordinary hero was a rape survivor.

Despite the reality that some tragedies are more horrible than others, upon reflection, she realized that suffering is suffering. It hurts no matter how it comes about. But she also recognized that most suffering people need to identify with others who have shared a kind of suffering similar to their own. Most of those on the program had attempted to reach out to help people much like themselves.

A comment one of the heroes made particularly struck home that day. "I knew if I sat at home and allowed resentment and anger to fester, or felt sorry for myself and decided life was not worth living, evil would win. I could not let that happen."

After watching that program, Nancy knew what she had to do. She had to seek God's help in *transforming her own season of grieving into a lifetime of caring.* At first she began to watch the news, and to make personal contacts with others who had been victims of crimes. Later she organized support groups for violent crime victims and their families which met in local churches, and set up a web-based support chat room.

Remembering that the crime which had destroyed her family could have been prevented if a prosecutor had not been guilty of misconduct, she began a campaign to change the laws in her state. The prosecutor's law license had been suspended for a year, because he had proceeded to trial in a capital case while intentionally concealing clear evidence of an accused man's innocence. The state Bar concluded the prosecutor had done this because he believed a guilty verdict would help him win an upcoming election. Despite the seriousness of the offense, the prosecutor had not violated any existing criminal law. Nancy fought to change that. She went to the legislature again and again, until legislation was passed providing criminal penalties for prosecutors who deliberately failed to follow the rules of discovery.

In the process, Nancy experienced healing. Somehow the deaths of her husband and child had meaning. Their loss was still inconsolable. Nothing would ever be as it was before. But Nancy now participated in the reality that evil does not have the final victory. She felt, within her being, that God had taken the horrific evil which was unleashed on her family, and somehow had transformed it into good. Because of the tragedy to her family, and her response to it, others were being comforted in their suffering, and some future tragedies were being prevented.

One Sunday morning, at the request of her minister, Nancy witnessed to her faith during morning worship. As she concluded her talk, she said, "I do not know any more today than I did then, why God does not prevent evil from happening. I have stopped worrying about that."

"What I know from experience is that God weeps when I weep.

God suffers when I suffer. And somehow, mysteriously, God works in me, and in so very many others who know life's tragedies, to turn suffering into service, and evil into good."

"When our Lord taught us to pray, 'Deliver us from evil,' I think he expected us to put legs on that prayer. He expected us to give our very best to that struggle. As I have studied the Bible and watched the news on TV, I have come to understand that God often looks around for some ordinary person who has experienced profound suffering in his or her own life, and calls that person to the work of transforming evil into good."

"It is not that God calls and then abandons us as we take up the task. Not by any stretch of the imagination. Psalm 22 begins with the words Jesus quoted on the cross, 'My God, My God, why have you forsaken me?'. But it does not end here. Later on in that Psalm we also find the words,

> *'For he has not despised or disdained the suffering of the afflicted one; he has not hidden his face from him but has listened to his cry for help.'" (Psalm 22:24)*

"God does not abandon us in our suffering, and God does not abandon us in our mission. God calls us, and through God's presence, God's power, God's compassion, God's healing, and God's leading, we are able to do far more than we ever could have imagined. And so I ask each of you, who may have been struck by some type of tragedy in your own lives, to hear God's promise today to God's people:

> *'We know that all things work together for good for those who love God, who are called according to his purpose.'" (Romans 8:28 NRSV)*

Chapter 10
When the Caterpillar Dies, the Butterfly Flies

"I have learned the secret of being content in any and every situation, whether well fed or hungry, whether living in plenty or in want. I can do everything through him who gives me strength." (Phil. 4:12b-13)

Affirmation

In the Peanuts cartoon created by Charles Schultz, Charlie Brown's favorite expression always has been "Good Grief!" Upon reflection, this exclamation may have appeared to us to be a strange combination of words. In light of a world filled with tragedies, we may have asked, " How can something caused by a terrible loss and accompanied by painful feelings ever be positive?" "How can grief be good?" Yet as we have seen in previous chapters, if we have accepted and lived our own journeys of grief as part of our journeys of faith, we have had glimpses of the goodness of grief all along the way.

Grief can be good, because it can soften the blow and ease our pain until such time as we are better able to cope with it. Grief releases the intense emotional pressure within which threatens to do long term damage to our emotions and bodies. Grief forces us to struggle for a time with our questions, our anger, our guilt, and our sorrow, so that we might reach the day when we will be free from their power over us. Grief can be good, because it can sensitize us to the suffering of others, awaken empathy, and call us to respond in service to the needs of our neighbors. And no matter how horrific a tragedy is, grief can become the means whereby God transforms evil in this world into good.

At a profoundly personal level, grief also can be good because it can lead us to a more mature faith and spiritual experience. It can transform our anxieties about living into genuine contentment. And it can guide us toward a life lived each day in the reality that *God is good all the time.*

CONTENTMENT

If we can see our journeys of grief through eyes of faith, we will see that there are important lessons to be learned. For example, as we saw with Rachel in Chapter 1, *our experiences of grief can teach us that our external situations are never our problem. Our problem is always to be found in the relationships we have toward them.*

Whether consciously or unconsciously, every difficulty confronts us with choices: "What is my attitude toward this going to be?" "Will I be resentful, bitter, and cynical?" "Or will I be humble, grateful, and life affirming?" "Will I focus on the negatives and limitations, or will I look for the positives and possibilities?"

It is clear the Apostle Paul understood that his situation was never his problem. As he faced persecutions and hardships, his relationship with Jesus Christ had given him the gift of contentment, no matter what was going on in his life. If he was well fed, that was, of course, fine. If he was hungry, that was no problem either. Paul had received the grace to be content with or without the comforts of life. And he desired that the members of the churches he had founded also would have that same contentment in the midst of their circumstances.

No matter how difficult and tragic our situations, our attitudes make a difference. Those who have survived concentration and prisoner-of-war camps have testified to the reality that survival under such horrible conditions often depends on people's attitudes. Those who continue to have faith, hold fast to their hopes, and are able to be compassionate toward others, are more likely to survive. And even those who do not survive, but who have possessed these same attitudes, can help to make survival possible for others.

Another lesson grief has to teach us is that there is no need, as they say, *to sweat the small stuff. Because tragedy separates us from someone or something precious to us, it can help us focus on what is truly important in life.* It can put into perspective the little daily aggravations of life. It can help us see the humor in our situations, rather than lose our serenity because someone or something has thwarted our self-wills. And it may assist us in detaching from our preoccupations with material possessions and our self-centered pleasures, and in refocusing on our relationships.

The loss of a parent, for example, may leave us lonely and longing for his or her company once again. But it also may motivate us to put more emphasis on spending quality time with our living loved ones. And it may compel us to focus on the reality of the way life is. In a few years, if not before, we too will die, as will all of our loved ones. As far as this world is concerned, we are, as the book of James says, "a mist that appears for a little while and then vanishes"(James 4:14b *NIV*). This awareness of mortality may help us to see every moment of life as a precious gift.

The death of a parent also may remind us that life is seasonal. It begins with the springtime of childhood and youth, continues through the summer of adulthood, the fall of mature years, and the winter of old age and death. Of course, death may come at any point along the way. But if we continue in each season, we are confronted with the question of the meaning and purpose of that season.

Each season of life holds new and difficult challenges. Our family and work responsibilities usually shift over time. And for persons of faith, our particular roles as servants of God may change as well. Sometimes we try to resist life's transitions. Yet we are given the choice to embrace the change and to know contentment, or to resist the change and miss the banquet that life is.

PURPOSE

The Psalmist tells us that after the long dark night of weeping, joy comes with the morning light. Dawn is the end of the night, but it also is the beginning of a new day. And every morning confronts us with decisions about what we are going to do with the gift of the day before us.

All periods of significant change are stressful times. This is so even when they are happy ones, as when a child is born. Much of our stress is rooted in the reality that major changes in our life situations usually require us to change as well. *When we encounter such turning points, we may find ourselves in need of discovering new purposes and new roles.*

This is especially true when we must start over after we have lost persons or circumstances which previously helped to define who we were, and what our lives were about. For example, some of us have spent months and even years providing care to loved ones. During those times, our care taking, for the most part, may have defined our reason for being. After our loved ones are gone, and no longer need our help, we may feel unsure about our roles in the universe. At such times, it is not unusual for us to feel a bit lost.

People whose lives previously were focused on making money and accumulating wealth and material possessions, also may feel the need to find new reasons for living. After a period of grief their old goals now feel empty and meaningless. They long for a fresh life direction that will make them genuinely happy and fulfilled.

If we are persons of faith, our general purpose is clear. We are, as Jesus indicated, to love God with our whole hearts, minds and strengths, and our neighbors as ourselves. To be about the love of God and neighbor is why we were created. That, of course, is what Jesus himself did. He went about being the love *for* God, and the love *of* God, in the world. And with the aid of the Holy Spirit, that also is what *we* are supposed to do with our lives.

Grief does not change our general purpose as people of faith. It may, however, challenge us to rethink what our individual and unique purposes might be. While for some this involves a particular personal calling, for many of us it has more to do with recognizing the gifts we have been given, even when they are modest ones. And it means deciding each day to be open to using our talents according to God's general purpose.

Furthermore, because of life changes, we may face new circumstances which prevent us from being faithful servants in the same ways as before. But we can be faithful servants nonetheless. A man who is housebound with a disability, for example, may not be able to be involved in the home construction projects of Habitat for Humanity as in the past. But he still may be able to use his computer to help with the organization's record keeping, fund raising, and publicity.

A woman who once gave significant sums of money to her church and to charities may not have the resources to continue that support. But she still may be able to provide substantial service to those organizations by donating her time and using her skills to help carry out their missions. A retired couple with health problems may no longer be able to participate in church and civic activities. But they still may be able to participate in their church's prayer chain and to spend time each day in prayer for others.

Even an elderly man bedridden in a nursing home can do more than wait to die. He can decide he will see each encounter with nursing staff and visitors as an opportunity to show appreciation and offer encouragement. And this can be done with a wink or a smile even when he is too weak to speak. *For as long as we have conscious life, we have the ability to allow God's love to flow through us to others.*

Joy

When we have reached the dawn of acceptance we face a new day. In fact, it is likely that we face many new days. And those days will pass, whether we live them as people of faith and according to God's purpose for our lives, or not. *If we have learned the lessons God wants for us to learn, as we have gone through the agony of the stages of our grief, acceptance has become for us far more than resignation, or even a calling. It has matured into the grace to embrace life as it comes to us each day.* And it is the assurance that God is good all the time, even when it does not feel that way.

When we are in the midst of our journeys of grief, we may not feel we will ever know joy again. Yet many who have walked the valley of sorrow before us testify to the reality that joy will return if only we allow it. If we have eyes to see, there are happy moments in each day. And there are times of joy in each season of life.

But for people of faith, joy is much more than this. The Apostle Paul wrote of a boundless joy in the midst of his troubles. *Joy is a feeling we possess in our hearts at all times, even when we are having the most difficult of days.* It does not depend on the successful pursuit of pleasure or material things. It is not conditioned upon whether life is going the way we wish it would.

The joy of our faith is a durable joy. It dwells within us at all times, because God's love dwells within us. It is a taste of that perfect joy we will know in the life to come. Death never can defeat us. Suffering and sorrow will end. And nothing ever will separate us from the love of God.

Alice

Despite their modest retirement savings, Alice and her husband Ed had retired early in order to spend time together. They moved from their large four-bedroom home, where their three sons had grown to maturity, into a two-bedroom house in a retirement community. For two years they enjoyed wonderful traveling adventures together. They visited Italy, took a Caribbean cruise, spent two weeks in Hawaii, and drove to a variety of places where they could enjoy the beauty of nature and entertaining events. Then Ed had a stroke and died.

Ed's passing understandably was devastating to Alice. They had married when she was only nineteen, and had remained together for forty-two years. They were not only husband and wife, but also were best friends. They enjoyed each other's company so much that they had little time or need to socialize with others.

Those two years of retirement had been magnificent. Despite her grief over Ed's death, Alice was very grateful to God for them. But after losing him, she felt lost. She grieved, as anyone would under the circumstances. What Alice felt was more than the normal sadness in losing such a close loved one. She felt her own life was over. So much of her identity had been tied up with his, that she did not feel like a person anymore. She felt empty and useless.

Alice and Ed had three sons. Each of them lived hundreds of miles away and had families of their own. After Ed's passing, Alice spent a week at each of their homes. All three sons and their families were pleasant enough, but during the visits Alice felt like a fifth wheel. As she flew home from the final visit, she wondered if it might have been more comfortable for her if one of her children had been a daughter. She sighed. The bond between mother and daughter would be something she would never experience. The visits had underscored the reality that her children had busy lives of their own and she would always feel like an intruder when she stayed with them. She knew future visits would be short and far between.

Alice had not been home more than a few days, when she received a call that her mother, who lived in an assisted living community, had fallen, broken her hip, and was in the hospital. Alice rushed to her side. After the surgery, Alice was told her mother would not be able to return to her previous residence, because she needed rehabilitation therapy and skilled nursing care. So upon her mother's release from the hospital, Alice arranged for her mother to be transferred to a nursing home near her own retirement community.

Over the next few months, Alice spent most of her non-sleeping hours at the nursing home. Her mother was ninety-two years of age, and the fall, followed by the surgery, weakened her already frail body. She was not able to get out of bed without being lifted and positioned by nursing staff. That activity was so painful for her that she soon refused their assistance, preferring to be bedridden. To make matters worse, an inflammation around the surgical wound was determined to be a treatment resistant infection.

Alice's mother now needed considerable assistance with her personal needs. And so Alice spent long and exhausting days as a caregiver. Sometimes when her mother was sleeping, Alice would escape to a bench in a peaceful garden courtyard between the nursing home units in search of a moment of serenity. It was there that she came to know Grace, an acquaintance from church, who was married to a man receiving care in the Alzheimer wing of the home. Although Grace was a few years older than Alice, and they had not known each other well before, the two women were drawn to each other's friendship. Over the weeks, they found themselves looking forward to those moments of respite, when they could sit outside on the bench together and chat about happier times.

Despite the dedicated and loving care of Alice and the nursing staff, the mother grew weaker every day. Her mother's constant pain became more severe, and frequent doses of potent pain medication were needed in order to make her reasonably comfortable.

Six months after the fall, in the midst of what seemed to be a period of interminable misery, Alice's mother developed pneumonia and had to be transported by ambulance to a local hospital. She was given major doses of antibiotics, but her medical condition continued to decline. Eight days after being taken to the hospital, with Alice faithfully beside her bed, she slipped into a coma.

During those difficult six months at the nursing facility, Alice's pastor had been diligent about visiting at least weekly and praying with mother and daughter. During the hospitalization he visited every other day. When her mother slipped into a coma, Alice called the pastor, and within an hour he arrived. As Alice's mother lay unconscious before him, Pastor Phil took hold of her pale small hand and spoke to her as if she were fully awake. "You are in a great position today," he said. "Maybe God will make you better, and you can spend a little more time here with this precious daughter you brought into the world, this one you love so very much, and who loves you just as much in return. Or perhaps God will take you away from her, and you can go to the other side, and you can be with all those loved ones who have gone before you. And there, all of you will rejoice because you have been reunited. Isn't that great? You are a winner either way." Then Pastor Phil offered a moving prayer while tears streaked Alice's cheeks.

A few hours after Pastor Phil left, Alice could hear her mother's breathing became labored and erratic. That night, as Alice sat quietly holding her hand, she felt her mother slipping away. The breathing stopped. The suffering finally was over.

Alice sat for a long time, before she notified the night shift. She was exhausted, deeply sad, and guiltily relieved. She tried not to think of what her own life was going to be like, now that her mother did not need her care any more. Instead, she began to think about the family and friends who would need to be notified, and she made a list of things to do, to carry out her mother's wishes at the funeral.

All three of Alice's sons flew in to attend the funeral of their grandmother, though they all decided to leave their busy families at home. Alice sat with her children and listened as Pastor Phil read the Scriptures, prayed, and offered his words of comfort and strength. Pastor Phil, as usual, had a lot of good things to say that day. But the words which meant the most to Alice, were the ones about the caterpillar and the butterfly.

"There is something ahead finer than we can dream of," Pastor Phil had said. "If a lowly caterpillar could talk, as he makes his way over twigs and stones, he would ridicule the idea that before long he will be a multi-colored butterfly, floating easily from flower to flower. But we know that when the caterpillar dies, the butterfly flies. He is changed from one kind of life and being, to a very different and more glorious kind of being. In a similar way, when our earthly phase is finished, God transforms us into our next phase, into life eternal, into a wondrous and glorious new being."

Alice thought about those earlier happier times when she had enjoyed watching the butterflies in her mother's flower garden. Her mother had loved butterflies. They were embroidered on her dresser scarves. She had ornamental butterflies hanging on her bedroom wall. She had pictures of butterflies displayed in her dining room. Alice also remembered enjoying the butterflies in the courtyard garden of the nursing home. Alice found great comfort in the pastor's words.

But as Alice tried to get back to a normal life after the death of her mother, she found herself perpetually perplexed. She did not know what *normal* was supposed to be any more. After all, normal once had been raising the boys, working as a bookkeeper at a local hardware store, and being a good wife. After retirement, normal was spending every possible moment with Ed. Then after her mother's fall, normal meant spending every possible moment providing care for her.

Now that she was alone again, Alice felt empty and useless. To make matters worse, she began to develop some health problems of her own. Her blood pressure shot up during the time she was taking care of her mother. She needed new crowns on her teeth, and one of her eyes was starting to develop a cataract. She could not hear as well. Her shoulders hurt from arthritis. It seemed that every few months she developed an additional diagnosis, and with it she added more pills to her daily medication box.

In the midst of these difficulties, Alice could not get the images of her mother's decline out of her mind. One day a great sorrow came over her, like a tidal wave. She wept for hours, until she cried herself to sleep. Alice had shed a lot of tears over the past months and years, but this was different. Her sorrow was not about losing what had been, but about the losses to come. Her mother's journey through old age, sickness, and death had given Alice a profound visualization of her own future.

Someone at the nursing home had a sign on the wall that read, "Old age is not for sissies." "How true!" Alice thought. She also remembered something she had read a long time ago, that old age was one of the tragedies of life which had troubled the young prince who would later be called the Buddha. Alice never had thought of old age as a tragedy, at least not until recently. But now, Alice understood she had wept deeply about her life because she was experiencing a tragic awareness of her own mortality. She was weeping over what aging already was taking from her, and over the anticipation of the suffering which often comes toward the end. "I hope when the time comes," she thought, "I go suddenly. I don't know if I can stand to go through what my mother went through."

With the burial of her mother behind her, Alice tried to get some order and routine back in her life. She went to church on Sundays, ate lunch by herself at one of the two tea rooms in town most weekdays, and went out for dinner with Grace on Thursday evenings. Over long talks while visiting at the nursing home, the two women had come to trust each other, as they openly discussed their personal difficulties. Now they both cherished those Thursday evening dinners together.

Grace could not help but notice Alice's darker than-usual-mood when they met at the restaurant one Thursday a few months after Alice's mother died. In her usual soft, caring voice, Grace gently asked, "What's going on?" "You don't look like you feel so well,"

"It shows that much, does it?" Alice responded. "I think I'm OK, but I'm depressed and I just feel so lost. I miss Ed. I miss my boys. I miss Mom. And I just feel useless. My life used to have a purpose. Now I only exist. I feel like I'm just getting up and going through the motions, every day. I don't want to be like this, but I don't know how to change it. You seem to be handling things pretty well, all things considered. How do you do it?"

Grace replied, "Well you have been through a lot lately, so don't be so hard on yourself for being in the dumps. Some days I wake up and think about what has happened to my life, and to my husband, and I can hardly get through the day. But most days, I remember I must still be here for a reason. And so, I try to take it one day at a time and see if I can figure out why the Lord has given me that day."

"I felt some of that, when I was still taking care of Mom. But now that she's gone, I don't seem to have a purpose any more," Alice responded. "Life is hard. Nothing really brings me much joy these days. All I can think about is that I am getting older and older and more useless all the time."

"Just listen to yourself." Grace interrupted. "That is quite a pity pot you are sitting on. Look, you may not be as healthy as you used to be. None of us are. You may have lost your mother and your husband. But you still have family, even if they live a long way from here. You still have your life, and you haven't lost your mind, as my husband has. So maybe its time for you to figure out what God wants you to do with this season of your life, besides sit around and wait to die of old age."

Alice was stunned. It was the first time Grace had spoken anything other than kind, gentle words. But she knew Grace was right. She just didn't know how to do anything about it.

"I guess I don't think I have anything to offer any more," Alice said, despondently. "I don't have any real talents to offer. The only things I ever have been good at were balancing books, taking care of my children, being a good wife to Ed, and being a good daughter to my mother. I know a lot of people my age volunteer to be leaders in the church, or in other kinds of groups. But that is just not who I am. I never have been good at that sort of thing. I know some people have hobbies, like painting pictures and making quilts, but I don't have any hobbies. I suppose I should think about volunteering to help out at the nursing home, but I don't think my nerves could stand it, now that Mom is gone. It would be too depressing for me. I think I am a pretty useless human being."

Returning to her usual comforting tone, Grace replied, "Nobody says you have to do any of those things. Let's see if we can figure out what God really wants you to do. From what you have told me, I see the seasons of your life like this. In the first one, God's assignment for you was for you to grow into maturity, to get a good education, to develop character and compassion, and to be a good daughter and friend. In the next one, God's assignment was for you to be a good wife to Ed, and to be a good mother to your children. You were faithful to Ed and supported him in what he was doing, as he loved and supported you. You had the assignment of delivering your children to adulthood and maturity as persons who would be self supporting, good citizens, as those who would know and serve God and make a positive contribution to the world. In the third season, while you continued to grow in your relationship with Ed, you became a bookkeeper at a hardware store, and you had the assignment to be an honest and good employee who made a contribution to that business, while saving for your retirement with Ed.

Then, in the next season of your life, you were taken on a roller coaster. First you had the gift of joy, of sharing wonderful experiences with your husband. Then you had the assignment to care for your elderly and infirm mother. Do you think that pretty much describes what God's plan has been for you till now?"

"Yes, that pretty much says it all," Alice responded.

"Now, I suspect you have entered a new period," Grace continued. "So what does God have in mind for you now? Look, you say you have no talent and you have nothing to offer. But look at what you have offered others, all those years. You seemed to have handled those assignments in excellent fashion. The common thread of what your life has been about, over the years, was your family. And now I believe you have something to offer your family, something that only someone of your age and experience can offer."

"And what, pray tell, is that?"

"Wisdom. You have wisdom. And your children and grandchildren need that wisdom. You know one of the things I think is wrong with our culture? We don't honor the wisdom of those with age and experience. In some cultures, when you get gray hair, you are honored. The elders are considered the keepers of the wisdom necessary for the good of the tribe or community. Our society, on the other hand, worships youth and inexperience. But that doesn't mean we should submit to that foolishness and keep silent. When we get old, we may not have the strength, or health, to contribute the way we were able to when we were younger. But we have knowledge, and we have wisdom the emerging generations need. And it is our assignment from God to see that they get it."

"So you think I should become some kind of meddling old fool?"

"Oh no! Not at all! What you need is to determine some ways that will communicate your wisdom effectively, so the next generations will have it when they need it, or when they are able to appreciate it, even if that's after you're gone."

"So, how do I do that?"

"Well let's start with this. What do your children and grandchildren know about their family heritage? What do they really know about you and Ed, and what life was like before they were born? Do you have any old family pictures?"

"I have boxes of them stored in the guest room closet. Some of them were Mom's, and some were from Ed's family. And, of course, lots of them are from when our kids were growing up."

"And what do you think will happen to all those precious pictures after you are gone?"

"They probably will be stored in somebody's home, and they could be lost or destroyed. I doubt if the boys will recognize many of the people in the old pictures."

"Well," Grace asked, "don't you think your family needs to have those pictures in a format which will allow them to understand and experience their heritage?"

As Alice drove home and prepared for bed, she felt an excitement for the first time in a long time. There just might be a purpose for her life, after all. As she lay awake thinking about the evening's conversation, and her role as keeper of the family heritage, she resolved first to have all the family pictures converted to digital images so they could be preserved on disk. Then she would sort them and arrange them into photo albums, labeling and identifying the people, times and places of the pictures. Then it occurred to her that no one had yet put together a genealogical record of the family. She would need to get started on that. There were family stories her father and mother had told her, and stories she had to tell of her own childhood and youth. These were interesting snippets from the past, and some of the stories contained life lessons, learned the hard way and worth sharing.

Some time in the middle of the night, when Alice got up to go to the bathroom, she found herself thinking about writing a book to record those family stories. Then her children and grandchildren could learn about their heritage. "When they're ready, when the time is right," she thought, "they'll want to know. And it is my assignment to make sure their heritage is not lost." Because the book would be of interest only to the family, she knew it would need to be self-published. But that would be a good use for the small inheritance she had received from her mother's estate. There was so much to do now. Alice was worried there might not be enough time to do it all.

Many years later, when Alice was bedridden in the same nursing home that had cared for her mom, her son Ed, Jr., sat by her side. While she was sleeping, he noticed a book sitting next to a stack of photo albums on the dresser. He reached for the book. It had a rough blue cover adorned with a large smooth image of a black and yellow butterfly. He opened the book, turned to the Introduction, and began to read.

"At my mother's funeral, my pastor spoke of the transformation of a caterpillar to a butterfly. He spoke of this as a symbol of the change from life in this world to eternal life. It does that for me, as well. But the butterfly also reminds me of the changes required of each of us as we advance through the seasons of life to which God has appointed us."

"In each season, God has assignments for us, no matter what our condition. In my golden years, God assigned me the joyful responsibility to pass to you, my children and grandchildren, the stories that will help you know how life was lived by those who came before you, and how you came to be who you are today. In doing this, I have tried to pass along some of the wisdom I learned from those who are no longer with us."

"If you will read this book and let the pictures, stories, and sayings of those who gave you life live in your hearts, your lives will be richly blessed by them. I pray each of you will find God's purpose for you at each season of your life. And when you get old, as I have gotten old, you will remember, if you are still here, that God is not through with you yet. And if, as you read this book, you think God is through with me, don't be too sure. I can't wait to find out what my assignment will be in Heaven."

Epilogue

The stories in the previous chapters were constructed from bits and pieces of the lives of real people who have touched my life over the years. The main story lines reflect the actual life crises of specific persons. The individual characters and narrative events used to convey the stories generally have been composed from the journeys of more than one person. Names and identifying information have been altered to protect anonymity. Most of the dialogue is fictional, and is intended to serve the dramatic purposes of the chapters.

More than three decades have gone by since my son's onset of schizophrenia. During the first several years, Mark was trapped in a revolving door between home and psychiatric hospitals. Local appropriate community based services were virtually non-existent for persons with Mark's diagnosis.

In 1984 I attended a state organizational meeting of the National Alliance on Mental Illness (NAMI). As I drove home from that meeting I felt I was being called to a ministry of advocacy, and I soon threw myself into the work of NAMI. I served as the executive director of the organization for six years before going to work for the state Division of Mental Health, Developmental Disabilities and Substance Abuse Services.

NAMI helped to bring attention to the problems of persons with serious mental illness in our state, and, in time, community services began to appear. Eventually, the impact on Mark's life was dramatic. He would have other crises. But he also had long periods of stability. At the time of this writing, he has experienced only one brief hospitalization during the twelve most recent years, and is participating in the benefits of housing and day programming primarily made possible by NAMI advocacy.

Through the years, since the onset of my son's mental illness, I have experienced several other life-changing times of grief. The final year of the last millennium was a particularly tough one. The responsibility of being the director of a state mental health, developmental disability, and substance abuse service system, with inadequate resources to serve the need, and never-ending governmental turbulence, was, by its nature, a difficult assignment. But in 1999, it was especially so, due largely, I believe, to political circumstances beyond my control. More significantly, it was a profoundly sad year for my family. My mother was diagnosed with cancer, and died five months later. Mark, caught his hand in a wood splitter and had to have it reattached. My father-in-law, who was also my close friend, dropped dead of a heart attack. And my dear mother-in-law, who declined rapidly in health after the death of her husband, also passed away a few months later.

The experiences of that year, and the other seasons of grief I have known along the way, have not been nearly as difficult, however, as the early years of my son Mark's mental illness. I believe that is true largely because God has changed me over the years, as God has changed the lives of countless other persons of faith who also have faced personal tragedies.

For me, and for the people who inspired the writing of this book, life-changing tragedies offer the opportunity, however painful, for faith to mature and deepen. When naïve faith no longer can serve as a kind of talisman to ward off bad experiences, authentic faith calls us to live in God's real world, and to accept and affirm the reality of our suffering. God does not prevent bad things from happening to people of faith. But God does abide with us, and God does suffer with us, when such things happen. Our journeys through the dark shadows are paved with moments of grace, if only we have eyes to see them. And, mysteriously, God is able to transform the evil that befalls us into good, if only we open ourselves to God's guidance. In faith we are assured, no matter what else befalls us, that God is for us, God is with us, and God will never abandon us.

My hope and prayer is that this book will help you, reader, on *your* journey of faith, to affirm with me the words of the Psalmist,

> *The Lord is close to the brokenhearted*
> *And saves those who are crushed in spirit.*
> *(Ps. 34:18 NIV)*

John Baggett

LaVergne, TN USA
21 October 2009
161635LV00001B/1/P